COUNTRY INTEGRATED DIAGNOSTIC ON
ENVIRONMENT AND NATURAL RESOURCES FOR NEPAL

MAY 2020

ASIAN DEVELOPMENT BANK

ADB

ISBN 978-92-9262-167-4 (print), 978-92-9262-168-1 (electronic)
Publication Stock No. TCS200118-2
DOI: http://dx.doi.org/10.22617/TCS200118-2

Note:
In this publication, "$" refers to United States dollars.

On the cover: Nepal has grown significantly and developments take into consideration the importance of environmental conservation and cultural heritage (photos by Kiran Pandey, Madhup Shrestha, and Narendra Shrestha).

CONTENTS

TABLES, FIGURES, AND BOXES

FOREWORD

Nepal is endowed with natural resources, diverse ecology and rare species of flora and fauna. A large part of the rural population in the country depends on these resources for livelihood. These precious natural assets are in a critical state of degradation from the impacts of natural calamities and human induced activities. Despite its negligible contribution to global greenhouse gas emission, Nepal is one of the most vulnerable countries to the impacts of climate change. The increasing greenhouse gas emission and the resulting global warming had triggered serious climate change impacts causing huge human and economic losses in the country in the past.

With the long-awaited political stability and the federal system of governance in place, Nepal is at a historic point to bring about economic and social transformation. The country is striving to eliminate poverty and expedite the pace of economic growth. Rapid infrastructure development to increase productivity and to provide access to social services is on top of the government development agenda. However, there is a growing concern that Nepal's desire for rapid development may come at the cost of environment. In order to protect its valuable natural resources, Nepal must strike the right balance between development and conservation. While this may seem challenging, especially given the limited capacity at the local levels, it is still possible with the right set of plan, policy and investment frameworks.

The 15th plan of the Government of Nepal prioritizes environmental conservation and increased resilience to natural hazards and climate change in its development efforts. Strategy 2030 of the Asian Development Bank (ADB) aims tackling climate change, building climate and disaster resilience, and enhancing environmental sustainability as one of its key operational priorities. ADB's new country partnership strategy 2020-2024 (CPS) for Nepal is aligned with the government's 15th five-year plan and the ADB's Strategy 2030. Accordingly, the CPS has focused on achieving environmental sustainability and resilience as one of its priority objectives.

ADB prepared this Country Integrated Diagnostic on Environment and Natural Resources (CIDENAR) for Nepal in order to identify issues, analyze causes, recognize challenges and prepare measures to protect environment and mitigate climate change and disaster risks in the overall development initiatives aimed by the new CPS. The measures for environmental conservation and risks mitigation considered by the CPS was founded on the overarching principle of integrated green growth and sustainable development.

The CIDENAR was prepared through wide consultations with local and national level stakeholders, development partners, academia and experts focusing on environment, natural resources and climate change issues. I would like to thank the stakeholders who provided relevant feedbacks that greatly helped in CIDENAR preparation. I would also like to commend the author and his team for preparing this diagnostic document which provided valuable inputs to the new CPS for ensuring environmental protection and resilience to achieve sustainable development goals.

Mukhtor Khamudkhanov
Country Director
Nepal Resident Mission

ACKNOWLEDGMENTS

The Asian Development Bank (ADB) prepared the Country Integrated Diagnostic on Environment and Natural Resources (CIDENAR) for Nepal. The report aims to mainstream environmental protection, climate change mitigation, and disaster risk management in ADB's country partnership strategy 2020–2024 for Nepal.

Deepak Bahadur Singh, senior environment officer, ADB Nepal Resident Mission, authored this publication with the support of Salil Devkota and Surya Man Shakya, ADB's environment consultants. Sharad Bhandari, principal economist, ADB South Asia Department, guided the CIDENAR preparation. Bimal Babu Khatri, associate safeguard analyst, ADB Nepal Resident Mission, assisted in publication of the CIDENAR.

ABBREVIATIONS

ADB	Asian Development Bank
BCM	billion cubic meters
BRBIP	Bagmati River Basin Improvement Project
CIDENAR	country integrated diagnostic on environment and natural resources
CPS	country partnership strategy
DFID	Department for International Development of the United Kingdom
EIA	environmental impact assessment
EU	European Union
FDI	foreign direct investment
GDP	gross domestic product
GHG	greenhouse gas
GLOF	glacial lake outburst flood
ha	hectare
IEE	initial environmental examination
IFAD	International Fund for Agricultural Development
IGG	Inclusive Green Growth
JICA	Japan International Cooperation Agency
LAPA	local adaptation program of action
MOFE	Ministry of Forest and Environment
MoPE	Ministry of Population and Environment
MW	megawatt
NAPA	National Adaptation Program of Action
NGO	nongovernment organization
NPC	National Planning Commission
REDD	Reduce Emissions from Deforestation and Forest Degradation
SASEC	South Asia Subregional Economic Cooperation
SEA	strategic environmental assessment
SDC	Swiss Agency for Development and Cooperation
SDG	Sustainable Development Goal
SNV	SNV Netherlands Development Organization
UNDP	United Nations Development Programme
USAID	United States Agency for International Development
WWF	World Wildlife Fund

A section of rural road which considers environment and heritage (photo by Kiran Pandey)

EXECUTIVE SUMMARY

A. Background

Nepal's Country Integrated Diagnostic on Environment and Natural Resources (CIDENAR) for Nepal aims to support the mainstreaming of environmental protection, climate change mitigation, and disaster risk management in ADB's new country partnership strategy (CPS) for Nepal, 2020–2024. The CIDENAR reviewed Nepal's environmental situation, including existing institutional and legislative provisions; the country's status toward achieving the Sustainable Development Goals; and the key challenges in creating environmentally sustainable, climate-friendly, disaster-resilient, and socially inclusive economic growth. ADB carried out an extensive consultation with relevant stakeholders including policymakers, government staff, development partners, academia, international and local nongovernment organizations (NGOs), and the media on priority issues hindering sustainable development and measures to address them. The consultation process has yielded a broad list of the causes of environmental degradation, including those that are common and specific to different sectors. This report analyzes the interlinkages among the causes and mitigation measures, and provides recommendations to address sustainable development challenges at the national level, and suggests ADB's relevant interventions through the Nepal CPS by considering the complementarity and harmonization among the plan, policy and strategy of the government and ADB.

B. Broad Findings

Nepal has recently transformed its governance system to a three-layer federal republic. The newly formed institutions in the provincial and local levels have critical deficiency in staffing, capacity, and resources to follow the path of sustainable development. Nepal has also been identified as one of the least developed countries in the world with a per capita gross domestic product (GDP) of $1,036.5

in 2019. The newly elected government is pursuing an accelerated growth path to make Nepal a middle-income country by 2030. Around 18.7% of the population is below the poverty line in 2018, and the government's target is to reduce this to 13% by 2022 and 4.9% by 2030.[1] Poverty in Nepal is concentrated in rural areas where agriculture is the main source of livelihood of almost 60.4% of the country's population. The poorest of the poor typically live on steep slopes under the constant risk of landslide, or in the low-lying, flood-prone areas; and they are weak in resources and capacity to recover from the impact of a disaster. While people living in poverty are seldom the cause of environmental damage, they often bear the outcome of it, which pushes them further in a downward spiral of the poverty trap.

Nepal has a unique young Himalayan geology, varied ecosystem with rich natural resources, abundant water, fertile land, and diverse sociocultural milieu—giving the country a huge potential for socioeconomic transformation. However, sustainable management of these resources has remained the main challenge. The young mountain geology, fragile ecosystems, poverty, lack of capacity and resources, and weak governance have made the country extremely vulnerable to environmental degradation and impacts of climate change and disaster risks. The climate change-driven events such as melting glaciers, degrading and eroding watersheds, drying water sources, and extreme precipitation pose a grave risk to Nepal's economy, and could cause losses equal to almost 2.2% of the country's annual GDP by 2050 and 9.9% by 2100.

C. Key Environmental Challenges

After a political transition and election of a stable government, Nepal is aiming for fast economic development and prosperity. The government aims to achieve this goal primarily by tapping the country's vast potential for hydropower, tourism, and natural resources. Currently, the scale of foreign investments in Nepal

---

1 Government of Nepal, National Planning Commission.2018. *Fifteenth Plan Approach Paper.* Kathmandu

is scant. But the interest and growth in foreign direct investment (FDI) is impressive in the last few years. According to the Central Bank of Nepal, the foreign investors from 39 countries have invested in 252 firms in Nepal with FDI stock of NPR137.7 billion as of mid-July 2016. The amount is 6.1% of the GDP. The outstanding FDI was highest in the service sector (70.2%). In March 2019, Nepal organized an investment summit where the world's business community committed investments in various projects with signing more than a dozen deals mainly in the hydropower and service sectors. This suggests no immediate threat for environment from highly polluting industries. However, compliance with environmental safeguards could get sidelined in a rush to increase the pace of development for rapid prosperity of the country. Overlooking environmental sustainability could later cause serious impacts with high economic loss.

(i) Poverty. The poor and vulnerable are more exposed to the risks of environmental degradation, climate change, and disasters. They get dragged into the downward spiral of poverty for not being able to cope with and recover from the impact of natural hazards. To survive, they have no other option but to exploit the available natural resources—further damaging the environment causing forest degradation and encroachment, water pollution, poor sanitation, and air and waterborne diseases. Hence, poverty and weak capacity to develop resilience to disasters are some of the major challenges in addressing environmental degradation in Nepal.

(ii) Risk of Climate Change. Although Nepal has a negligible contribution to global greenhouse gas emission (0.027%), it faces serious impacts of climate change on lives, properties, infrastructure and the local economy. Climate change-driven events could cause losses equal to almost 2.2% of annual GDP by 2050 and 9.9% by 2100. Scientists have predicted that Nepal would experience increasing trend of frequent extreme climatic events, such as cloud bursts and severe floods, increased drought, high temperature and rapid glacial retreat. The poor would become more vulnerable to these events. The impacts of climate change could jeopardize the huge investments

made in infrastructure, cause watershed degradation and serious water crisis, reduce agricultural productivity, and increase vulnerability from natural disasters.

(iii) Increasing Disaster. Nepal is exposed to a variety of natural hazards and human-induced disasters. More than 80% of Nepal's total population is at risk from natural hazards, such as floods, landslides, windstorms, hailstorms, fires, earthquakes, and glacial lake outburst floods (GLOFs). Nepal is among the 20 most disaster-prone countries in the world. In part, this is because Nepal is in a seismically active zone with high probability for massive earthquakes. Nepal ranked fourth out of 124 countries in 2017 in terms of climate risk, according to the Global Climate Risk Index, which assesses the impacts of meteorological events in relation to economic losses and human fatalities.[2] Also, the country ranks 11th in terms of global risk for earthquake and 30th in terms of flooding.[3] Out of the 21 cities around the world that lie in similar seismic hazard zones, Kathmandu is at the highest risk in terms of impact on people.[4]

(iv) Rush Syndrome to Expedite Prosperity Goals. The newly established elected government has carried the citizens' aspiration for quick economic development and prosperity. The government has a long-term vision of bringing the country to the status of high- income, developed nation by 2043, and aims to achieve the ambitious average economic growth rate of 10.3% during the plan period (fiscal year 2019/2020 to 2024/2025). Since the opportunity for industrial development seems to be limited, the path to attain prosperity will be through hydropower, tourism, and use of natural resources. To harness the water resources, the government aims to generate 3,000 megawatts (MW) hydropower over the next 3 years; 5,000 MW in 5 years; and 15,000 MW in 10 years;[5] and 40,000 MW of power through hydro and renewable energy in 25 years.[6] The government is also trying to attract higher FDI. In a rush to increase the pace of development to achieve prosperity, the safeguards agenda could get sidelined, and could later cause project-specific, cumulative, and transboundary impacts with high economic costs.

---

[2] D. Eckstein, M. Hutfils, and M. Winges. 2018. *Global Climate Risk Index 2019: Who Suffers Most from Extreme Weather Events?* Berlin: Germanwatch e.V.
[3] Government of Nepal, Ministry of Population and Environment et. al. 2016. *Nepal Earthquake 2015: A Socio-Demographic Impact Study.* Kathmandu.
[4] Government of Nepal, Ministry of Home Affairs, UNDP et.al. 2019. *Disaster Risk Reduction in Nepal: Status Report.* Kathmandu.
[5] Government of Nepal, Ministry of Energy, Water Resources, and Irrigation. 2018. *Government White Paper on Energy, Water Resources, and Irrigation.* Kathmandu.
[6] Government of Nepal, National Planning Commission. 2019. *15th Plan Approach Paper (2020–2024).* Kathmandu.

(v) Newly Established Federal Government.
The constitution has given the role and responsibility of local infrastructure development to the provincial and local governments. However, they lack capable human resource for environmental governance. The communication and coordination among local and central environmental agencies have several gaps. The weak institutional capacity to plan, implement, monitor, and enforce safeguarding of the development works poses huge environmental risks. The over-extraction of riverbed aggregates and quarries on fragile slopes, pumping of groundwater in urban areas (such as in Kathmandu Valley), open disposal of solid waste and sewerage, unplanned land use change, and destruction of green cover are a few examples of increasing environmental degradation. Over exploitation of natural resources has been rampant. Personal and political interests—such as the local governments aiming to increase tax by issuing licenses for the extraction of natural resources—have seriously ignored the huge environmental cost incurred from over exploitation due to insufficient monitoring and enforcement. An indication of greater environmental damages could be construed from the recent report of Nepal's Center of Investigation for Abuse of Authority (CIAA), which cautions that the case of fiduciary risks has geometrically increased at the local levels.

(vi) Risk of Remittance-Steered Economy and Unplanned Urban Sprawl. The rural population benefits from a remittance-based income that contributed 25.4% of Nepal's GDP in 2019.[7] Much of the money flowing into the rural areas is used to buy consumer goods, land, houses, and vehicles, and to settle family matters. They tend to migrate to nearby towns to seek better social services. Following the formation of local and provincial governments, unplanned and unsafe semi-rural townships have started to emerge attracting the remittance-supported internal migrants from the adjacent rural catchments—and this situation results in higher environmental risks. Migration from rural to urban areas has increased pressure on land and water in the towns, and agricultural lands and forests are being encroached and converted into built-up areas. These settlements lack proper urban amenities such as safe drinking water,

sewerage system, and roads. The migrants ultimately end up living in highly polluted, unhygienic, and shanty settlements in environmentally high-risk areas.

(vii) Environmental Degradation of Chure. The highly fragile Chure hills—as a water source and a natural resources basket—is the lifeline of millions of people living in the area and those at the downstream in the Terai plains. However, Chure's ecosystem is seriously damaged by the pressure of human activities, such as deforestation, mining of riverbed and fragile slopes, erosion from haphazard construction of non-engineered rural roads, and unscientific agricultural practices. These activities have resulted in serious watershed degradation, landslides, erosion, and waterbody sedimentation—aggrading riverbeds in Terai and causing frequent floods. The drying of water sources is causing migration of settlements and desertification of the fertile agricultural land of Terai. To address environmental degradation, the government prepared the Chure Conservation Master Plan, which needs an investment of $2.5 billion over a 20-year period.

D. Inclusive Green Growth

ADB prepared the Environmental Operational Directions 2013–2020 to promote transition to inclusive green growth (IGG) in Asia and the Pacific and address the causes and consequences of climate change and natural hazards. This CIDENAR proposes four mutually supportive IGG strategies for consideration in ADB-supported project design and operation: (i) promoting the shift to sustainable infrastructure, (ii) investing in natural capital, (iii) strengthening environmental governance and management capacity, and (iv) responding to the climate change imperative. The green growth concept is not meant to replace sustainable development, but it is an approach through which the aim of sustainable development could be achieved. Hence, this CIDENAR recommends measures for the new CPS to adopt in the areas of environmental protection, climate change adaptation, and disaster resilience by mainstreaming ADB's IGG operational directions and Strategy 2030, and the government's periodic plan and program in the future ADB support.

---

[7]   ADB. 2020. *Nepal Macroeonomic Update April 2020*. Kathmandu

E. Recommendation for the Country Partnership Strategy

With the new CPS, ADB will focus on large infrastructure development, and improvement in sustainable and resilient development in Nepal through improved governance in the newly established federal governance system. The CPS stresses the importance of environmental sustainability given Nepal's rich and diverse natural resources and fragile geology, and the need for resilience to climate change and natural disasters. In this regard, the CIDENAR supports the mainstreaming of the following recommendations in the CPS.

(i) Improved Environmental Governance

- Update old standards, policies, acts, and regulations and harmonize them among the three levels of government to make the development investments environment friendly, climate proof, and disaster resilient.
- Institutionalize safeguards in all the three levels of the government and provide support through staffing, resources, and capacity building. ADB will continue supporting the safeguard sections established in the government departments and authorities implementing infrastructure such as the urban development, water supply and sewerage, hydropower and transmission lines, roads and airports, irrigation, and local infrastructure development.
- Explore possibility to implement the national pollution control strategy and action plan, which was prepared under ADB support.
- Support in integrating and implementing the strategic environmental assessment (SEA) as part of national environmental protection act and regulation. Coordinate the conduct of SEA of hydropower policy (proposed from energy sector portfolio), Integrated Water Resource Management (IRWM) policy {proposed through Bagmati River Improvement Project – Additional Financing (BRBIP-AF)}, transport master plan (proposed from transport sector portfolio), irrigation master plan, and urban and/or municipal development plans (through ongoing Regional Urban Development Project).
- Promote non-motorized transportation, greening of roads with biodiversity-friendly approaches (wildlife crossing, fish survey, tree counting and plantation,

watershed conservation), and use noise barriers {through road master plan, South Asia Subregional Economic Cooperation (SASEC) Road Connectivity Project, SASEC Roads Improvement Project, SASEC Highway Improvement Project, and the proposed SASEC Mugling–Pokhara Highway Improvement Project - Phase I}.
- Promote regional cooperation in transboundary biodiversity conservation.
- Coordinate with development partners to activate the environment and climate change thematic groups for Nepal to share, coordinate, and generate synergy.

(ii) Sector Recommendations Based on Inclusive Green Growth Principles

a. Sustainable Natural Resources and Land Use Management

1. Combat watershed degradation

- Provide support in controlling deforestation, forest encroachment, habitat stratification particularly by linear projects (road, canal, transmission lines), and uncontrolled mining. Support watershed improvement (through ongoing Bagmati River Basin Improvement Project, Building Climate Resilience of Watersheds in Mountain Eco-Regions Project, Bagmati River Basin Improvement Project - Additional Financing; and roads, hydropower, and transmission line projects).
- Address human-induced environmental degradation, and disaster risks posed by over-exploitation of Chure and the impacts of climate change.
- Explore possible support by accessing climate change and disaster risk reduction funds to implement the Chure Conservation Master Plan.

2. Sustainable use of natural resources

- Promote community-based watershed management and promote the reduction of emissions from deforestation and forest degradation to conserve and enhance forest carbon stock (ongoing Bagmati River Basin Improvement Project, Building Climate Resilience of Watersheds in Mountain Eco-Regions Project, Bagmati River Basin Improvement Project - Additional Financing, and Tanahu Hydropower Project), in addition to the projects in ADB investment pipeline.

- Support all three levels of government in preparing legal and institutional mechanism to protect natural resources and prevent unsustainable extraction of riverbed material and exploitation of natural resources.

3. Biodiversity Conservation
- Update hydropower policy and establish a method of estimation of minimum environmental flow at the downstream of dams with support from energy portfolio.
- Establish a baseline of fish and their lifecycle movement in the integrated river basins, identify strategic locations for dam, and declare rivers to be left undisturbed and guarded as national park, to protect aquatic biodiversity (through energy portfolio or explore funds for a technical assistance.
- Promote forestry and ecotourism for biodiversity conservation through participatory approach (through SASEC Road Connectivity Project, SASEC Road Improvements Project, SASEC Highway Improvement Project, Tanahu Hydropower Project, SASEC Power System Expansion Project, SASEC Power System Expansion Project – Additional Financing, Tanahu Hydropower Project, and the proposed priority river basin flood risk management project, in addition to other projects in the ADB investment pipeline under urban, roads, and energy portfolio).

4. Integrated Water Resource Management
- Adopt IWRM policy, act, and regulation and conduct SEA.
- Establish river basin organization for integrated management of the basin.

5. River Conservation
- Invest in reviving highly important but ecologically dead rivers such as those in Kathmandu Valley and other urban centers through sewerage management, river flow augmentation and riverbank beautification (through Bagmati River Basin Improvement Project and the proposed Bagmati River Basin Improvement Project-Additional Financing, Melamchi Water Supply Project, Kathmandu Valley Water Supply Improvement Project, Kathmandu Valley Wastewater Management Project, and Regional Urban Development Project).

- Support watershed management and riverbank flood risk management in vulnerable river basins (through the proposed Priority River Basin Flood Risk Management Project).

(iii) Sustainable Infrastructure Development

a. Common to All Infrastructure
- Provide support through technical assistance projects using climate change funds in updating design standards to mainstream climate change impacts in the design and implementation of infrastructures.
- Make environment management plan requirements always as part of tender document with cost listed in the bill of quantities. Include detailed and clear safeguard clauses such as reward and punish mechanism in the contract agreement. Support the preparation of a standard list of environmental safeguards and include the list in bill of quantities with rate estimation and contract agreement clauses (through PID/Kathmandu Upatyaka Khanipani Limited, energy, and urban portfolio).
- Employ mandatory submission of site-specific environment management plan among contractors for employer's approval prior to mobilization in the field. Support in preparation of a simple template for site-specific environment management plan as a guideline for contractors.
- Make compensatory plantation mandatory. Support the establishment of nursery at provincial and local levels and prepare a guideline for tree counting and plantation. Update bio-engineering manual prepared by Department of Road for use by other sectors.
- Support in producing trained and skilled bioengineering technicians (through ADB's Capacity Development Resource Center and the proposed Bagmati River Basin Improvement Project-Additional Financing, and Rural Connectivity Improvement Project).

b. Sustainable Transportation
- Update the Nepal Road Standard 2014 and regulation and the rural road standard and regulation to encourage non-motorized transport infrastructure (cycle track, walkways, footpath, zebra crossings, overhead crossings); link shortest travel routes; green roads and highways through mandatory trees plantation based

- on road category; and use noise barriers and road signage, information board, and delineators.
- Promote modes of transport with low energy emission such as electric vehicle, energy- efficient infrastructure, and railways and waterways.
- Prioritize water management, spoil disposal, and bioengineering for slope stabilization, particularly in rural roads. Blacktop rural roads.
- Support the local government in adopting a policy to restrict non-engineered rural road construction by using heavy machineries and closing the roads for heavy vehicles over 1 ton and tractors during monsoon on earthen roads (through rural connectivity improvement project).

c. Sustainable Urban Development
- Support the formulation of harmonized urban development policy and legal provisions among federal, provincial, and local governments (through regional urban development project).
- Implement national pollution control strategy and action plan.
- Prepare urban development master plans for rapidly developing towns to avoid growth of unplanned and shantytowns (through regional urban development project).
- Reduce GHG and air pollution by translocating polluting industries, shifting to energy efficient and electric vehicles, promoting the use of bicycles, and managing solid waste (through South Asia Tourism Infrastructure Development Project, SASEC Road Improvement Project, SASEC Highway Improvement Project).
- Raise public awareness on environment friendly urban practices such as integrated solid waste management and sanitary landfill sites.

d. Clean Energy Development
- Avoid ad hoc placing of dam on rivers seriously affecting aquatic life (through technical assistance support, Tanahu Hydropower Project, proposed Dudhkoshi Hydropower Project).
- Scale-up shifting of energy modes using low carbon emission alternative sources (through SASEC Road Improvement Project, SASEC Highway Improvement Project).

- Promote clean energy generation by promoting alternative energy sources.
- Use existing or single transmission line corridor with multiple stringing instead of constructing multiple parallel lines through forest and other sensitive areas. Conduct SEA of Transmission Line and Hydropower Master Plan.

(iv) Responding to Climate Change Imperative
- Support in updating policies, acts, regulations, and strategies on climate change.
- Strengthen institutional structure and public sector capacity in mainstreaming climate change risks in the project cycle across the three levels of government.
- Add and upgrade the hydrometeorological stations, and improve the technical quality of data collection using state-of-the-art technology (through the proposed priority river basin flood risk management project).
- Invest in applied research on economic footprint of climate change on national economy.
- Scale-up the shifting of energy modes to low carbon emission alternative sources and accelerate off-grid renewable energy solutions (such as solar, wind and mini-hydropower) in remote rural areas.
- Promote watershed conservation to maximize carbon sequestration and market them internationally as environment services (through Bagmati River Basin Improvement Project and Building Climate Resilience of Watersheds in Mountain Eco-Regions, and other roads and energy projects).
- Seek partnership with development partners and explore climate change support funds to leverage investments in climate change adaptation and resilience building.

(v) Disaster Risk Management
- Formulate "hard" and "soft" structural measures and non-structural measures (such as flood forecast and early warnings) and policy instruments for water induced disaster risk reduction and management (through the proposed Priority River Basin Flood Risk Management Project, Tanahu Hydropower Project, and the proposed Dudhkoshi Hydropower Project).

- Institute a risk-informed development and mainstream disaster risk reduction and climate change adaptation in sector development planning.
- Support the construction of safer schools with "build back better" principle (through Disaster Resilience of School Project).
- Support in ensuring improved access to remote areas in the event of disaster (through Rural Connectivity Improvement Project).

- Set up an effective disaster information management system (DIMS) at the central and provincial levels as a one-stop information hub.

(vi) Knowledge Management

- Document and share good practices and lessons learned from past experiences and replicate good practices drawn from country and regional experience.

I. INTRODUCTION

A. Study Background

The new country partnership strategy (CPS 2019–2024) of the Asian Development Bank (ADB) and Nepal has taken into account environmentally sustainable and climate-change and disaster-resilient development for ADB-supported programs and projects. ADB support will be guided by Safeguard Policy Statement (2009) and Strategy 2030, and aligned with the environmental protection provisions of the Government of Nepal. This Country Integrated Diagnostic on Environment and Natural Resources for Nepal (CIDENAR, also referred to as "the study") has been prepared to assess Nepal's current environmental context; identify key issues and challenges through integrated inter-sectoral approach; and recommend measures to mainstream environment, climate change, and disaster risk management in ADB operations. The CIDENAR has drawn its analysis, findings, and recommendations from the following:

- The State of Environment of Nepal and the Compendium of Environment Statistics Nepal 2019 published by the Nepal Central Bureau of Statistics;
- Nepal Country Environment Note 2014 prepared by ADB;
- Policies, legal provisions, guidelines, and documents in relevant sectors published by the Government of Nepal, ADB, and development partners;
- The Sustainable Development Goals and the areas of development stated in the five-year periodic and interim development plans of Nepal;
- ADB's Environmental Operational Directions 2013–2020: Promoting Transition to Green Growth in Asia and the Pacific;
- ADB's Nepal Country Partnership Strategy (2013–2019) and the Country Operations Business Plan 2018–2020 and 2020–2022;
- Other publications of the government and development partners; and
- The Lao People's Democratic Republic's CIDENAR.

B. Contemporary Development Narrative

Nepal has met some of the Millennium Development Goals targeted for 2015; however, the results were not consistent across different social groups, gender, and geographical regions. To fill the Millennium Development Goals gaps, Nepal has also adopted the SDGs to be achieved by 2030. Nepal has transformed its governance system into three-tier federal governance—designating 7 provinces, 293 municipalities, and 460 rural municipalities. The election of all three levels of government concluded in 2017. The newly elected government having comfortable majority at all the three levels of government have raised prospects toward greater political stability and accelerated economic and social development. Nepal is now targeting to graduate from the rank of lower middle-income country by 2030; however, among other challenges, the impact of climate change and disaster risks are becoming the major factors impeding the development investments of the country.

Climate change has emerged as the foremost global challenge. The erratic climatic behavior with change in precipitation, droughts, floods and landslides, and the rapidly melting glaciers have indicated uncompromising environmental, social, and economic impacts on the development endeavor of Nepal. The greenhouse gases (GHGs) and the short-lived climate pollutants, such as black carbons, are believed to have contributed to increased global warming—although Nepal's contribution to world GHG emission is negligible. Since the causes of climate change are transboundary in nature, the efforts of Nepal are insufficient to reduce the global GHG emission. Yet, the country has the potential to meaningfully contribute to reducing the global carbon emission through a shift to clean and renewable energy and forest conservation.

Nepal is listed as one of the world's most disaster-prone countries and has experienced frequent natural hazards causing high economic and human losses. A combination of fragile geology lying on the thrust line of Indian and Tibetan tectonic plates, steep and fragile topography, and intense impact of monsoon rain, exacerbated by the impacts of climate change, has made the young Himalayan geology highly vulnerable. The most common natural hazards in the country are fire, flood, and landslide. Periodic earthquakes cause huge impact on human life and damage of infrastructure.

The quality of infrastructure in the country needs improvement to withstand not only natural vulnerabilities but also embed green concepts in development planning and operation. Additionally, appropriate and sustainable development management is required to prosper the country's tourism, agriculture, and water resources based on social, environmental, and economic values.

C. The Study Approach

The study was primarily based on available secondary information and extensive consultations with relevant stakeholders including policymakers, experts, academia and development partners. The root causes for degradation of environment and the increasing climatic and disaster risks were identified and analyzed. Based on the analysis and findings, the study offered general and CPS-specific recommendations to follow a sustainable and green growth path of development.

II. THE ENVIRONMENTAL CONTEXT

A. Global Environmental Context

Human civilization and globalization are known to be the dominant reasons of constant change in the global environment. Various processes contribute to global environmental problems, such as pollution, global warming, ozone depletion, acid rain, depletion of natural resources, increase in population, unmanaged waste generation and disposal, deforestation, and loss of biodiversity. One of the major impacts the earth confronts is the release of large quantities of carbon dioxide and other greenhouse gases in the atmosphere as a result of industrialization and urbanization, which consumes fossil fuel at an unprecedented rate. Loss of forest, damage to the ecosystem of water bodies, over-exploitation of natural resources, rapid extinction of species due to habitat destruction, and other well-known causes are connected to global environmental degradation.[8]

The United Nations Development Framework has aimed to achieve the Sustainable Development Goals (SDGs) since 2015, and states that the SDGs are the blueprint to achieve a better and more sustainable future for all. They address the global challenges, including those related to poverty, inequality, climate change, environmental degradation, prosperity, and peace and justice. The scientific research and findings carried out by various national and international agencies indicate that climate change will eventually increase the frequency and severity of extreme weather events in Nepal, leading to various types of natural hazards.

In addition to the SDGs, the Paris Agreement on Climate Change and the Sendai Framework for Disaster Risk Reduction are important international frameworks that drive action toward climate change and disaster risk management (DRM). Multilateral environmental agreements provide a basis for promoting environmental sustainability and sustainable development.[9] The members of the Organisation for Economic Co-operation and Development and developing countries are working together toward achieving sustainable growth and carbon neutral development.

B. Environmental Goals of Nepal

Nepal has attempted to incorporate environmental concerns into development processes over the last 2 decades by promulgating the National Environment Policy and Action Plan 1993, the Environment Protection Act 2019, and the Environment Protection Regulation

Figure II-1: **Three Dimensions of Sustainable Development**

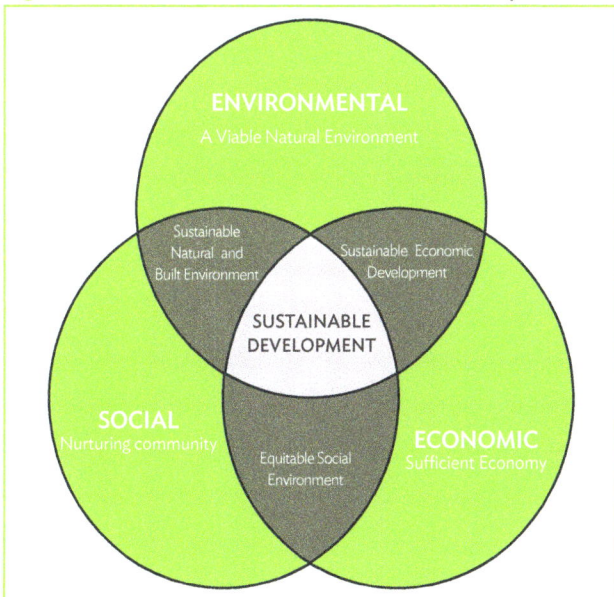

Source: https://www.quora.com/What-are-the-advantages-of-sustainable-development

---

[8] R.L. Singh, ed. 2017. *Principles and Applications of Environmental Biotechnology for a Sustainable Future.* Singapore: Springer Science + Business Media. https://link.springer.com/book/10.1007/978-981-10-1866-4

[9] More than 500 international agreements on global environmental protection and management are currently in effect. Examples are the Ramsar Convention on Wetlands of International Importance (1971), the Convention on International Trade in Endangered Species of Wild Fauna and Flora (1973), the Convention on Transboundary Air Pollution (1979), the Montreal Protocol on Ozone Protection (1985), the Basel Convention on Control of Hazardous Wastes (1989), the Convention on Biological Diversity (1992), the Convention to Combat Desertification (1994), and the Ozone Depleting Substances Consumption Rule 2001.

1997 (draft environment protection regulation 2019 is under approval process). The act was promulgated in October 2019 by replacing old act of 1997. The new Act and Regulation has included the new challenges posed by climate change and disaster risks.

Previous studies and reports suggest that Nepal's major environmental problems have bearing on both the natural process and human-induced activities. Deteriorating air quality, drying up of water sources and depleting groundwater, pollution of surface and groundwater, over-exploitation of natural resources, deforestation, unmanaged solid waste, increase in emission of toxic pollutants, loss of biodiversity, unscientific agricultural practices, and harmful land use changes have been some of the major causes of environmental degradation. Some of the root causes of rapid environmental degradation are weak monitoring and enforcement, weak institutional capacity, scarce resources in public institutions, and inefficient interagency coordination.

The impacts of climate change have become one of the critical environmental phenomena in Nepal. Drying up of water sources resulting in mass migration of entire villages (cases in Jajarkot and Mustang districts), unprecedented rainfall causing devastating flash flood (2008 Koshi flood in eastern Nepal) and massive landslides (2014 Jure landslide in central Nepal), desertification and decrease in agricultural productivity, and the spread of new diseases are all causally connected to the impacts of climate change. Nepal has prepared a climate change policy, implemented institutional reforms, organized awareness programs, and attracted various international funds to implement climate change adaptation and disaster risk reduction programs. The international agencies are also supporting the government in carbon trading in international market.

The 14th National Development Plan of Nepal (2017–2019) and the 15th National Development Plan Approach Paper (2020–2024) have envisaged the legal and institutional reforms for green growth and climate-resilient development. Both plans seek to protect the environment by developing climate smart villages, improving environmental assessment and conducting strategic environmental assessment (SEA), minimizing climate change risks through adaptation and resilience program, improving hydrometeorological forecasting system, and developing and/or improving surveillance and management of disasters, such as flood, fire, and glacier lake outburst flood. The government has also drafted a national strategy to reduce pollution.[10]

Although Nepal has made good progress toward achieving its Millennium Development Goals (MDGs), its progress in Goal 7 (environmental sustainability) requires improvement. The Nepal Multiple Indicator Cluster Survey conducted by the Central Bureau of Statistics indicates that the targets for environmental sustainability and global partnership were not fully achieved.

Nepal's overarching sustainable development goal by 2030 is to reduce poverty and ensure basic livelihood facilities for the present and future generation and offer opportunities for the citizens to participate in social, economic, political, cultural, and ecological development (footnote 10). The key SDGs related to environment are:

(i) 95% of households have access to piped water supplies and improved sanitation, 100% free of open defecation, and 100% urban households connected to a sewerage system;

(ii) 99% of households have access to electricity, 10% of the households use firewood, generate 3,000 MW in 3 years, 5,000 MW in 5 years and 15,000 megawatts of hydropower in 10 years, and limit fossil fuel consumption to 15% of total energy consumption;

(iii) increase forest cover to 45% and protected areas to 25%; and

(iv) undertake climate action for minimizing the impacts of climate change.

---

[10] Government of Nepal, Central Bureau of Statistics. 2015. *Compendium of Environment Statistics Nepal.* Kathmandu.

C. Economy, Poverty, and Environment of Nepal

1. Macroeconomy

Nepal is considered a least developed country, with a per capita gross domestic product (GDP) of $1,036.50 in 2019. The government is pursuing an accelerated growth path for Nepal to become a lower middle-income country by 2030.[11] Over the last two and a half decades, Nepal has made considerable progress in reducing absolute poverty. The decline in poverty was due to remittance, increasing wage rates, improved access, and increasing active population.[12,13] However, the country continues to face regional, rural-urban, and social disparities. The incidence of poverty in rural areas inhabited by 81% the population in 2011 had about twice as high as in urban area. Poverty among socially disadvantaged groups such as Dalits, Madhesis, Muslims, and indigenous Janajatis is significantly higher than the national average.

The macroeconomic statistics released by the Central Bank of Nepal indicates foreign investors from 39 countries have invested in 252 firms in Nepal with FDI stock of NPR137.7 billion as of mid-July 2016. The amount was 6.1% of the GDP. The outstanding FDI in Nepal was highest in the service sector (70.2%), followed by industry and agriculture sectors. Communication, financial intermediation, education, hotels, and restaurants were the dominant investments attracting FDI. Although hotels and restaurants attracted only 2.2% of the service sector FDI, increase in the number of tourists has encouraged investments. The share of FDI in industry was 29.5% in mid-July 2016. In the industry sector, hydropower and manufacturing industries (cement, paints, beverages, and steel rebar) were the main subsectors receiving FDI. The agriculture sector attracted only 0.3% of FDI, which is nominal.[14]

Nepal's unique geological setting, rich natural resources, abundant water, fertile land, and cultural diversity form a sound basis for the socioeconomic development of the country. However, sustainable use and management of these resources has been a challenge. Even the modest economic growth achieved over the past decades has come at a high environmental cost. Soil erosion and degradation, declining soil fertility, Nepal's monsoon-dependent agriculture, the improper use of fertilizers and pesticides, increasing temperature, variation in precipitation, and frequency and intensity of droughts and floods have reduced agricultural production.[15]

According to the foreign trade statistics provided by the Department of Customs, the trade deficit in the country increased by 13.55% (NPR1,321.42 billion) in the fiscal year 2018/2019. The economy is characterized by low productivity resulting in low economic growth and inadequate number of good jobs. Insufficient and basic standard of infrastructure, uncompetitive business environment, and weak governance and institutional capacity underpin low productivity and competitiveness of the economy.

Despite these constraints, Nepal has the potential to deliver higher and more inclusive growth by properly utilizing the huge hydropower potential, irrigation, medicinal herbs, and tourism. Agriculture has high potential if year-round irrigation could be provided in arable land, and if productivity is increased and transformed into commercial high value products.[16] In March 2019, Nepal organized an Investment Summit attended by more than 700 delegates from 40 countries signing 15 new deals and memorandums of understanding. Besides, the country also received 17 applications for 10 projects. This indicates that the country aims to achieve prosperity by mobilizing the private sector including foreign investment; although, most of the committed

[11] ADB. 2019. *Nepal-Macroeconomic Update - 2019*. Kathmandu
[12] Government of Nepal, National Planning Commission. 2007. *Three Year Interim Plan* (2007/2008–2009/2010). Kathmandu.
[13] World Bank. 2008. *Strengthening Institutions and Management Systems for Enhanced Environmental Governance*. Report No. 38984-NP 2008. Kathmandu.
[14] Nepal Rastra Bannak. 2018. *A Survey Report on Foreign Direct Investment in Nepal*. Nepal.
[15] Japan International Cooperation Agency (JICA). 2012. *Review of Food Production and Agriculture in Terai– JICA's Support Strategy*. Kathmandu.
[16] ADB, DFID, and ILO. 2009. *Nepal: Critical Development Constraints*. Manila.

investments are in hydropower and service sectors rather than in other seriously polluting industries. Nevertheless, environmental challenges are expected to increase along with the size of investments.

2. Poverty Incidence

The relationship between population and environment is generally viewed as complex. The growing unemployment is responsible for fueling the poverty crisis in Nepal. According to the Nepal Labor Force Survey conducted by the Central Bureau of Statistics in the last fiscal year 2017/2018, the unemployment rate in the country has reached 11.4% compared to total labor force. The population growth rate of Nepal was 1.7% in 2018. The poverty rate fell from 41.8% in 1996 to 30.9% in 2004, and 25.2% in 2011. The 15th plan approach paper envisages to reduce population below poverty line from current 18.7% to 11% during the plan period. In 2015, Nepal formulated its first national population policy in 2015 (footnote 10). The population growth puts stress on natural resources and biodiversity because of increased human demand leading to degradation of soil and watershed, deforestation, commercialization of land, and exploitation of natural resources.

The country ranked 147th of 189 countries in the global human development index in 2018. The nominal per capita gross domestic product (GDP) grew from $498 in 2009 to $1,004 in 2018.[17] There is a wide variation in poverty between urban and rural areas and across geographical regions. Poverty in Nepal is mainly a rural phenomenon with approximately 75% of the population and 90% of the poor population living in villages with agriculture as their main source of living. Poverty incidence in urban areas is almost 23%—lower than in the rural areas. The differences can also be seen in terms of ecological zones.[18] The disparity in poverty levels is evidenced by non-monetary indicators of welfare, such as health outcomes, human poverty indices, and subjective poverty rates. Dalits (socially excluded indigenous communities) and women suffer more from poverty compared with other social groups. Gender inequality is high, with the country ranking 101 out of 149 countries in the 2018 gender inequality index.[19] Studies indicate that the poor and the vulnerable live in more inaccessible and unsafe areas with higher disaster risks,

Box II-1: Correlation between Poverty and Ecosystem Protection.

Studies have shown that environmental protection initiatives can help alleviate poverty. For example, a study done in Costa Rica revealed that eco-tourism efforts contributed 66% decrease in poverty levels in regions situated near protected parks and natural areas due to economic opportunities provided by tourism. Paul Ferraro, professor of economics and environment policy in Georgia State University recommends three triggers that show a direct correlation between poverty reduction and environment conservation: (i) changes in tourism and recreational activities, (ii) infrastructure development (road, water supply, health clinic, schools), and (iii) changes in ecosystem services (crop pollination, nutrient cycle). Hence, the net impact of ecosystem protection was to alleviate poverty due to tourism revenue and job creation.

Source: https://borgenproject.org/how-protecting-the-environment-alleviates-poverty/

and they have minimal capacity to build resilience from natural hazards and disasters. The government has set a target of reducing poverty by one third over the next three years. Around 21% of the country's population is below the poverty line, and the target is to reduce this to 13% by 2022. A draft policy prepared by the Ministry of Land Management, Cooperative and Poverty Alleviation aims to bring down the poor population to 5% by 2030 (submitted for cabinet approval).

The interrelationship between poverty and environmental damage is complex and is heavily influenced by a range of social, economic, cultural, physical, and behavioral factors. These include the ownership of or entitlement to natural resources, access to common resources, strength or weakness of communities and local institutions, individual and community responses to risk and uncertainty, and the way people use scarce time are all important in explaining people's environmental behavior.[20] Box II-2 illustrates this environment and poverty/vulnerability nexus

---

[17] United Nations Development Programme. 2019. *Nepal Human Development Report.* New York.
[18] ADB. 2016. *Asian Development Outlook 2016: Asia's Potential Growth.* Manila.
[19] World Economic Forum. 2018. *The Global Gender Gap Report.* http://www3.weforum.org/docs/WEF_GGGR_2018.pdf
[20] World Health Organization, Commonwealth Secretariat. 1991. *HIV/AIDS Community-Based Care and Control.* Kampala.

Box II-2: Poor in Nepal

- Of the total poor, more than 90% live in rural areas. People in the mountains are poorer than people in the Terai.
- Lower caste people and women are poorer than higher caste people and men.

Source: Global South Development Magazine. 2017. Poverty in Nepal: Causes and Consequences. Finland

where environmental entitlements are mediated by the "internal" factors of environmental change, environmental management practices and poverty/vulnerability, and the impact of "external" processes. Poverty and environment are closely interrelated. While the poor are seldom the principal creators of the damage, they often bear the brunt of environmental damage and are often caught in a downward spiral of poverty.

The poor in large cities faces greater health risks and threats from environmental hazards and suffer from inadequate housing, poor sanitation, polluted drinking water, and lack of other basic services. It is the poor who depend most on natural resources for their livelihoods, and who suffer most from the impacts of climate change, deforestation, landslides, floods, and other environmental problems. A study by WWF-UK suggests that lifting people out of poverty would require conservation of the environment and natural resources they rely on; and the needs of people should be addressed in order to protect the environment. The reversal of vicious cycle of poverty and environmental decline requires rapid economic growth and closing of infrastructure gaps.[21]

Figure II-2: Vicious Cycle of Poverty and Environment Degradation in Developing Countries

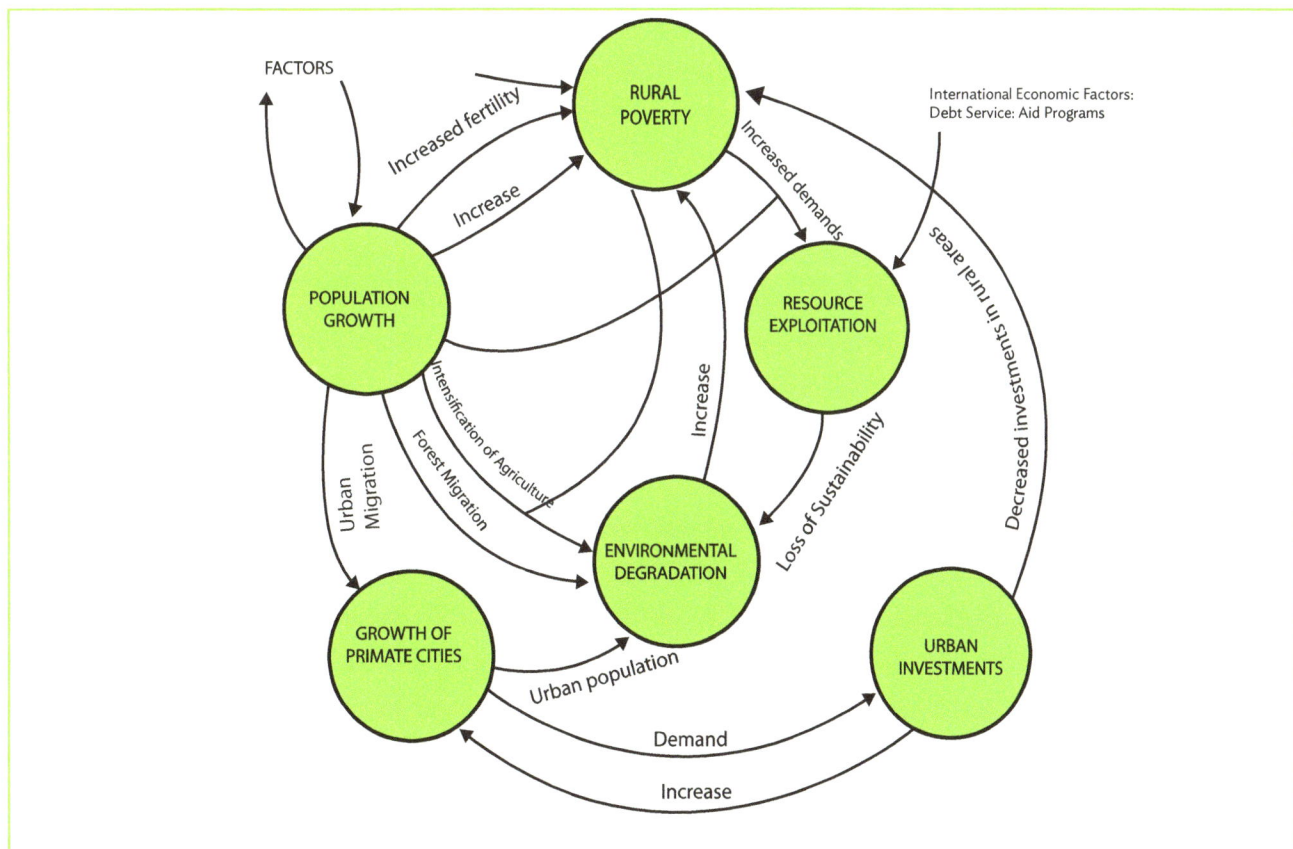

Source: UNESCAP. Poverty and Environment https://www.unescap.org/sites/default/files/CH09.PDF

---

[21]   R. Wichmann. 1995. The link between poverty, environment and development. *The political challenge of localizing Agenda 21. USA: National Center for Biotechnology Information, U.S. National Library of Medicine.* Countdown Istanb. 1995 Nov;1(5):1, 3-4.

3. Poverty and Disaster Risks

Evidence from around the world suggests that the poorest people are disproportionally affected by disasters. The poorest of the poor, who largely rely on agriculture, typically live on steep slopes under the constant shadow of landslides, or in low-lying flood-prone areas, and have virtually no resources with which to bounce back after a disaster. This makes it difficult for them to escape the poverty trap. Non-poor households often fall into poverty as a result of recurring natural hazards.[22] A vicious downward spiral is created, wherein poor individuals are forced to overuse environmental resources to meet their day to day need, and the ensuing degradation of their environment further impoverishes them, making their survival even more difficult and uncertain. The fast population growth has led to a rapid increase in demand for fuel wood, timber, fodder, and land to grow more crops.[23] The environmental implications are greatest when rapid change occurs in ecologically vulnerable urban or rural areas (poverty reserves).[24] The majority of the population affected by disasters has always been from the poorest communities. To increase production, poor farmers expand cultivation into highlands that are not suitable for agriculture. The result is accelerated soil loss, land degradation, declining productivity of farmland, and sedimentation in downstream areas. In many cases, communities that live in high-risk areas tend to have higher levels of poverty, and as a result do not have the ability to relocate to safer areas.[25] The living conditions of the poor are dire. Indoor cooking with firewood has a direct impact on health and is one of the causes of the extremely low life expectancy among women and children. Use of firewood also causes deforestation. In Nepal, the total expenditure on social protection is only around 2% of GDP, which places it among the countries with the lowest level of social protection.[26] Less than 50% of the amount goes to the poor. Hence, the poorest households need to rely on their own resources to recover from disasters and poverty.[27] Between 1980 and 2017, disasters in Nepal (floods, landslides, droughts, and earthquakes) led to about 21,000 deaths, affected the lives and livelihoods of almost 13 million people, and resulted in approximately $5.9 billion in direct physical losses.[28] The 2015 earthquake was estimated to have pushed 2% to 3.7% of the population below the poverty line.[29] Climate change impacts are already felt through watershed degradation, drying up of water sources, droughts, forest fires, and water-induced disasters, which further fuel the vicious cycle of poverty. [30]

[22] UNDP. 2009. *Nepal Country Report: Global Assessment of Risk*. Kathmandu.

[23] M.B. Poudyal Chhetri and A. Shakya. 1999. *Environmental Degradation in Nepal*. Disaster Preparedness Network and DUDBC. Kathmandu.

[24] UNDP and EU. 1998. *Poverty and Environment: Priority for Research and Development*. Institute of Development Studies. Sussex.

[25] UNDP, World Bank et. al. 1993. *Review of the Nepal Risk Reduction Consortium*. Kathmandu.

[26] Chandra Ghimire. 2019. *Social Protection in Nepal*. Kathmandu.

[27] S. D. Bhatta. 2009. *Analysis of the Relationship between Poverty and Disaster*. University of Illinois. Chicago.

[28] Guha-Sapir, D., R. Below, and Ph. Hoyois. 2018. *EM-DAT: The Centre for Research on the Epidemiology of Disasters and Office of Foreign Disaster Assistance of USAID International Disaster Database* (www.emdat.be). Universite' Catholique de Louvain. Brussels.

[29] Government of Nepal, National Planning Commission. 2015. *Nepal Earthquake 2015: Post-Disaster Needs Assessment, Key Findings*. (Vol. A). Kathmandu.

[30] ADB. 2014. *Assessing the Costs of Climate Change and Adaptation in South Asia*. Manila.

III. THE STATE OF ENVIRONMENT

A. Forest and Biodiversity

The total forest cover (forest and other wooded land) is 44.74% of the total land area of the country, of which 23.3% is protected area (national park, conservation area, and wildlife reserves).[31] The forest cover is 32% in Mid Hills, 23% in High Mountains, and 7% in High Himalayas. The total estimated carbon stock in Nepal's forest is 1,054.97 million tons (176.95 ton/hectare).[32]

Forests provide vital natural resources including fuelwood, timber, forage, medicinal and aromatic plants, and non-timber forest products, which are a major source of livelihood of the rural communities. They also contribute to the protection of watersheds, act as carbon sink, and help in regulating atmospheric conditions. From the southern plains of Terai to the northern Himalayas, forest types in Nepal comprise the tropical, sub-tropical broad-leaved, sub-tropical pine, temperate broad-leaved, temperate conifer, sub-alpine conifer, alpine scrub, and Trans-Himalayan steppe rangelands consisting of spiny dwarf shrubs.[33] In 2018, agriculture and forestry contributed 27.1% of GDP with direct products, and environmental services 27.5% of GDP; while forests supplied 78.14% of rural energy needs in the form of fuelwood.[34]

Recently, forest areas have been encroached for expanding farmland, settlement, and infrastructure development. Annual deforestation rate in Terai was 0.44% over 1999–2010 due to encroachment by urbanization, over grazing, invasive species, forest fire, and mining of sand and boulders. Forests in the middle-mountain are strongly impacted by infrastructure development, particularly rural roads. Fuel wood used for cooking has gradually gone down from about 70% of the total households in 2003/2004[35] to 64.4% in 2010/2011,[36] although use of fuel wood and animal dung for cooking is still prevalent in rural areas. Nepal lost 2.72 million hectares (ha) of forest with more than 10% crown cover between 1965 and 2013, with an average annual forest clearance of 56,710 ha. Of this total area, 1.76 million ha was degraded to shrub land.[37] Altogether, 0.96 million ha of forest and shrub land was estimated to have been lost to farming, urban expansion, and infrastructure development, or left barren. About 94,659 ha forest area is encroached by 121,234 households.[38] The rate of loss of forest is alarming; it has affected natural habitats, biodiversity, and ecosystems.

Despite rapid deforestation, Nepal has been successful in participatory forest management, and possesses 1.77 million ha of community forest and 5,696 ha of buffer zones around 13 protected areas.[39] A total of 2.23 million ha of forest lands (about 41% of the total national forest area including shrub land) were managed by 22,266 community forest user groups formed by 2.9 million households.[40] The forest conservation was effective as economic benefits to sustain rural livelihood dependency had been associated with the community forestry program. Local beneficiaries manage the forest and utilize forest resources in a sustainable manner, based on an annual plan approved by the district forest offices. Studies on community forestry's impact found out a reduction in fuel wood extraction among community forest user groups.[41] Community forestry has been favorable for ecosystem services provision, including greenhouse gas sequestration, timber forest products, and habitat for biodiversity. By 2025, the government aims to bring 2.3 million ha of forest

31 Government of Nepal, Ministry of Forest and Soil Conservation. 2016. *Forestry Sector Strategy*. Kathmandu.
32 M.K. Jhariya, A. Banerjee et.al. 2019. *Sustainable Agriculture, Forest and Environmental Management*. Singapore.
33 J. D. A. Stainton. 1972. *Forests of Nepal*; S. M. Amatya and K. R. Shrestha. 2003. *Nepal Forestry Handbook*. Kathmandu.
34 Government of Nepal, Ministry of Finance. 2018. *Economic Survey 2017/18*. Kathmandu.
35 Government of Nepal, Central Bureau of Statistics. 2003/2004. *Nepal Living Standard Survey*. Kathmandu.
36 Government of Nepal, Central Bureau of Statistics. 2011. *Statistical Database of Nepal*. Kathmandu.
37 Government of Nepal, Ministry of Forest and Soil Conservation. 1999. *Forest Resources of Nepal*. Publication No. 74. Kathmandu; HMGN/ADB/FINNIDA. 1988. *Master Plan for the Forestry Sector*, Nepal. Kathmandu; Government of Nepal. 2011. *Forestry Sector Policy*. Kathmandu.
38 Government of Nepal, Department of Forest. 2017. *Hamro Ban: Annual Report of the Department of Forest*. Kathmandu.
39 Government of Nepal, Central Bureau of Statistics. 2019. *Environment Statistics of Nepal*. Kathmandu.
40 Government of Nepal, Central Bureau of Statistics. 2019. *State of Environment Nepal*. Kathmandu.
41 T. Tachibama et. al. 2009. *Does community based management improve natural resources?* Evidence from the forests in Nepal. Kathmandu.

area under the community forestry regime, according to the Forestry Sector Strategy for Nepal (FSS 2016–2025). The Strategy aims to deliver five major outcomes ranging from sustainable production and supply of forest products; improvement of biodiversity, watersheds, and ecosystem services; increased contribution to national economic development; and inclusive and accountable forestry sector institutions and organizations to climate-resilient society and forest ecosystems.

The Forest Policy 2015 is the key policy guideline for conservation programs for forests, plant resources, wildlife, biodiversity, medicinal plants, and soil and watershed. The policy calls for sustainable and climate-resilient management of forest ecosystem and watersheds; and these should be sustainably managed through decentralized, competitive, and well-governed forest sector that provides inclusive and equitable income, employment, and development opportunities. The prevalent practice of aligning development infrastructures through forest area such as road, hydropower, transmission lines, and operation of mines are causing watershed degradation, forest fragmentation, loss of habitat, and barrier to wildlife movement. While rural roads enhance accessibility to the rural population, construction of non-engineered and haphazardly constructed earthen roads in hills by using heavy equipment caused adverse environmental consequences due to massive deforestation, forest habitat stratification, and instigation of landslide and erosion.[42] Uncontrolled forest fires, timber smuggling, and grazing in the forests are some of the threats against forest protection and watershed conservation. Forest encroachment due to rural-urban migration has become a major cause of loss of forest area. Learning lessons from the past, the government has declared working directives for offsetting forest clearance by development projects and enforcing them to plant trees at a ratio of 1:10 for each felled tree and guard them for five years. The lost forest area has to be replaced by the developer by arranging for an equal area of land in coordination with the district forest office.[43]

B. Ecosystem and Biodiversity

Of the total forest area of the country, 23.39% is declared as a protected area.[44] Various legal instruments guide ecosystem and biodiversity conservation, and protection of endangered flora and fauna.[45] Nepal is a party to over 22 international conventions including convention on biological diversity and a member of the Nagoya Protocol on access and benefit sharing. Nepal is also a member of the intergovernmental panel on biodiversity and ecosystem services. The government in 2010 declared Siwalik hills (Chure) which covers 12.78% of the area of Nepal as a protected area managed by the President Chure Conservation Development Committee formed in 2014. Chure is home for 14% of the country's population. However, deforestation and collection of riverbed aggregates in the fragile Chure hills (1.9 million has) have caused massive erosion, sedimentation of rivers in Terai causing flood, and loss of agricultural land and wildlife habitats. Uncontrolled livestock grazing and forest fires are also adversely affecting the forests. The region with 73.6% forest cover had an annual deforestation rate of 0.18% in 1999–2010. Destructive fishing, ad hoc placing and construction of dam across rivers, and wildlife poaching have threatened biodiversity conservation. Rhino poaching significantly declined to a single incident in April 2017 over the last 3 years. The tiger population has reached 235 according to the 2018 tiger census. The Nepal Army is guarding the national parks and wildlife reserves, and their wardens have authority to take action against offenders. Since the damage has been mostly due to human activities and infrastructure development, and not due to serious industrial pollution, it is still possible to reverse the ecosystem degradation in Nepal through sustainable development measures, awareness, investment in natural capital, minimized climate change risks, and improved environmental governance.

C. Land Degradation

The use of land and soil is very important in sustaining human life. More than 90% of the country's population depend on land for basic need. Land degradation involves reduction of the nature's capacity to provide ecosystem

---

42 SMEC International Private Limited and Cooma Australia Pvt. Ltd. et al. 1999. *EIA of Nepal Road Maintenance and Development Project*. Kathmandu.
43 Government of Nepal, Ministry of Forest and Environment. 2019. *Working Procedure with Standards for Use of Area in National Forest by National Priority Projects*. Kathmandu.
44 Nepal has declared 12 national parks, 1 wildlife reserve, 1 hunting reserve, 6 conservation areas and 13 buffer zones.
45 National Park and Wildlife Conservation Act 1973; Forest Act 1993 and Rules 1995; National Wetland Policy 2013; Buffer Zone Management Regulations 1996 and Guidelines 1999; Aquatic Animal Protection Act 1960; Standards for Removal of Forest Trees 2014; Use of Forestland for Other Uses 2007.

goods and services. Soil erosion is the main cause of land degradation. Soil erosion takes place due to unscientific farming on hill slopes, landslides, deforestation, livestock grazing, and rampant mining in the hills (footnote 35). Various studies indicate that the annual soil loss in Nepal ranges up to 105 tons per hectare with 34% water induced erosion, 60% mass wasting (geological erosion), and 3% wind erosion. Nepal has prepared the National Land Use Policy 2015, which aims to categorize land based on landform, capability, usability, and necessity (footnote 35). Other causes of land degradation in Nepal are land clearance, unplanned urban sprawl due to rural-urban migration, and depletion of soil nutrition due to poor farming practices. The maximum estimated soil erosion rate is very high in the Mahabharat Hill (6300-4200 ton/square kilometer/year).[46]

D. Water Resources and Energy

1. Water Resources

Nepal has a total drainage area of 194,471 square kilometers comprising more than 6,000 rivers.[47] The rivers flow from mountains in the north to hills and plains in the south, and finally discharges in the Ganges in India—contributing 47% of its monsoon flow. The rivers are of three types: (i) large snow fed rivers that originate from Himalayas and maintain reliable dry season flows, (ii) medium size rivers originating from the high hills (Mahabharat range), and (iii) small seasonal rivers originating from Chure, which dries in winter and brings devastating flash flood during monsoon. The ratio of wet (June–October) to dry period (November–May) discharge in the rivers in Terai plain is in the range of 8 to 14, indicating limited amount of water in the rivers during dry season.[48] Annual water flow in all rivers of Nepal is about 225 billion cubic meters (BCM), of which only 6.9% is utilized.[49] Other water bodies consist of 5,000 lakes; 1,380 reservoirs; and 3,808 glaciers with 1,466 glacier lakes. About 21 glacier lakes are identified with potential risk of glacial lake outburst flood (GLOF).[50] Nepal is also rich in groundwater resources with 11.5 BCM rechargeable reserve in shallow and deep aquifers (footnote 47), of which 5.8 BCM can be extracted annually without any adverse effects. Despite having large reserve, groundwater extraction is only 0.756 BCM for irrigation and 0.297 BCM for domestic use,[51] which is 17.8% of the potential. Groundwater is abundant and underutilized in Terai, whereas overextraction of groundwater has depleted groundwater table in cities, such as the Kathmandu Valley. Widespread water pollution has resulted in increased water scarcity, poorer public health, lower agricultural yields, and a declining quality of aquatic life in lakes and rivers. When forest area is lost, it causes watershed degradation, loss of biodiversity, landslides and erosion, frequent flooding, and diminished groundwater recharge. Farm livelihoods, including those of the poor, become precarious and the cycle of poverty is entrenched.[52]

Nepal lacks an integrated river basin planning and management system, scientific water pricing, and cost recovery mechanism. The country also lacks sufficient hydrometeorological network, resources for management of existing network, flood forecasting and warning systems, and geo-seismic database. Lack of environmental database and mapping, weak integration of environmental consideration in planning of water resource developments, poor implementation and enforcement of environmental impact assessment (EIA), and lack of strategic environmental assessment (SEA) for national plans and policies have constrained the policymakers to informed decision-making. Weak enforcement of surface and groundwater pollution, watershed degradation, and unsustainable water use, aggravated by the risks of climate change, have been the major reasons for depleting freshwater resources in the country.

2. Energy

The energy sources in Nepal are categorized as traditional, commercial, and alternative. Alternative energy is synonymous with new, renewable, and non-conventional form of energy. Traditional source of

---

[46] See footnote 10.
[47] See footnote 39.
[48] S.G. Shah and G. Singh. 2001. *Irrigation Development in Nepal: Investment Efficiency and Institutions.* Kathmandu: Winrock International.
[49] Government of Nepal, Ministry of Energy, Water Resources and Irrigation. 2018. *White Paper on Current Status and Future Roadmap for Energy, Water Resources and Irrigation Sector.* Kathmandu.
[50] ICIMOD, GFDRR, The World Bank. 2011. *Glacial Lakes and Glacial Lake Outburst Floods in Nepal.* Kathmandu.
[51] Government of Nepal, Water and Energy Commission Secretariat. 2005. *National Water Plan.* Kathmandu.
[52] ADB. 2001. *Water for All: The Water Policy of the Asian Development Bank.* Manila.

energy includes biomass fuels particularly fuel wood, agricultural residues, and animal dung used in the rural areas, which covers 70.47% energy consumption share. Energy from petroleum products covers 12.53%, and hydropower shares only 3.39% of the total consumption. The electricity demand in the country has far outgrown its supply capacity, leading to load curtailments and increased dependence on imports from India. The estimated peak demand in Nepal during FY2017–2018 was 1,500 megawatts (MW) as against the available capacity of 1,150 MW, resulting in a deficit of about 350 MW. About 63% of the population in Nepal has access to electricity, but the supply quality has been unreliable and inadequate. Nepal has long recognized that the development of its large hydropower potential is an important cornerstone for its poverty reduction and economic growth efforts. The power sector lacks adequate investment, partly due to poor regulatory and investment environment for private sector participation.[53]

In the past 4 decades, rivers in the Middle Mountains were dammed on ad hoc basis, mostly for generating electricity and irrigation. The country has the techno-economic potential of generating 43,000 MW of hydropower. However, the installed capacity of hydropower is 1,073 MW (562 MW by the Nepal Electricity Authority and 511 MW by private developers), and 450 MW is purchased from India to meet the demand of 1,300 MW. At present, 172 hydropower projects with 4,642 MW capacity are under construction and planning process. About 55 MW of renewable energy is being generated from alternative renewable energy sources. Eight renewable energy projects were registered under United Nations Framework Convention on Climate Change as carbon reduction projects earning NPR1,000 million under carbon trading.[54] Nepal aims to generate 15,000 MW energy by 2030. However, the hydropower policy lacks SEA for ensuring environment friendly development of energy sector.

3. Irrigation

The arable land in Nepal is 2.641 million has, of which 1.766 million has is irrigable and 1.433 million has is irrigated. Of the irrigated area, 0.443 million has is irrigated by groundwater, 0.168 hectare by farmers-managed irrigation systems, and 0.822 million has by surface water. Only one-third of the total irrigated area has year-round water availability for irrigation (footnote 51). In addition to rehabilitation of small-and-medium-scale, farmers-managed irrigation systems, Nepal is also constructing and operating a few major scale irrigation projects (such as Rani Jamara, Sikata, Bagmati, and Sunsari-Morang irrigation projects). Some are large-scale, multipurpose inter-basin water transfer projects (such as Bheri-Babai and Sunkoshi-Marin diversion projects). The World Bank and ADB are supporting the rehabilitation of farmers-managed irrigation systems. The country requires development of irrigation infrastructure to quickly benefit small and marginalized farmers and increase their socioeconomic condition, which could be achieved by rehabilitating their traditional small-and-medium-size, farmers-managed irrigation systems. On the other hand, large systems are needed for greater economic benefits and national food security.

The irrigation sector has good plans, policies, regulations, and working procedures. Some of the constraints faced by the irrigation sector in Nepal include weak institutional system and dependability syndrome of farmers on government support for operation and maintenance. Damage to systems generally occurs as a result of rainfall and landslides, degrading rivers due to over excavation of riverbed aggregates, and aggrading rivers in Terai due to sedimentation causing flood. Weak coordination between irrigation and agriculture agencies has always remained a major constraint to integrated development of irrigated agriculture.

E. Urban Development

The level of urbanization in Nepal remains low but the pace of urbanization has remained faster and is likely to remain so in the future. Only 17.1% of Nepal's population resided in 58 designated urban areas, according to the 2011 census. However, with the addition of 235 municipalities under the federal system, 19% of the population resides in 293 designated urban areas in 2019 (6 metropolis, 11 sub-metropolis, and 276 municipal councils). During the period 2001–2011, the population growth rate in urban areas was 3.4% per annum (3.2%

---

[53]   ADB. Concept Paper for Project No. 50059-003: Nepal - SASEC Power Transmission and Distribution System Strengthening Project. Unpublished.
[54]   See footnote 49.

Box III-1: National Urban Development Strategy 2017

The Strategy recognizes resilience as a guiding principle in planning and development of urban systems. Major strategies identified are promotion of multi-hazard approach to deal with disasters and climate change; internalization of resilience in land use regulations, building codes, and by-laws; and enhancing awareness and preparedness to deal with disaster risk at all levels of government, civil society, and local community.

Source: Government of Nepal, Ministry of Urban Development. 2017. *National Urban Development Strategy 2017*. Kathmandu.

during 2000-2017), compared with 1.4% per annum for the country as a whole.[55] The absence of stringent policies to regulate and manage this growth has resulted in haphazard development of municipalities and emerging towns. Municipal infrastructure has not kept pace with the rapid rate of urbanization, resulting in deficit of urban roads and footpaths; insufficient water supply, sewage, and drainage; improper solid waste management system; diminishing urban open space; and increasing squatters, and polluted rivers. Other areas of concern include increasing air, land, and noise pollution; growing urban transport with high fossil fuel consumption and GHG emission; land use incompatibility and public space encroachment; depleting cultural heritage and aesthetics; and increasing climate change and disaster risks. Traffic congestion is also worsening, especially in the Kathmandu Valley, where public transportation system is still rudimentary. The population grew by an annual rate of 6.6% in the Kathmandu Valley during 2001–2011, making it the most affected part of the country.[56] Most of the municipalities have more rural than urban characteristics. The haphazard and unregulated development of urban areas has worsened the communities' exposure and vulnerability to natural hazards, given the high risk of earthquakes in the country.

F. Pollution

The vehicular emission, brick kilns, and unmanaged construction in urban areas are the major contributors of dust and GHG emission. According to the Global Environmental Performance Index 2018, Nepal ranked last out of 180 countries on poor air quality. The existing systems of air and water quality monitoring are weak. Dust and vehicular emissions are the major air pollutants in urban areas. Poor traffic management, poor vehicle maintenance, and the use of adulterated and sub-standard fuel exacerbate air pollution. Burning of biomass is a major cause of air pollution in rural areas. The ambient air quality measured in major urban areas indicates high levels of PM_{10} (particulate matter), TSP (total suspended solids), and SO_2 (sulfur dioxide) against the WHO and Nepal standards.[57]

The government monitors air pollution at a limited extent especially in urban areas although they have prepared a modest set of national standards and institutional mechanism.[58] The government plans to install air pollution monitoring stations in 56 different locations in Kathmandu Valley. Studies show increasing air pollution levels in major urban centers—particularly dust particles and black carbon. The $PM_{2.5}$ and PM_{10} levels are much higher than the minimum national standards. Indoor air pollution is prevalent and especially high in the rural areas where biomass is still predominantly used as cooking fuel. According to the data from the Department of Transport Management, the number of vehicles registered in the country has reached 2,551,138 units and motorcycles 1,998,283 units, which are mostly concentrated in Kathmandu Valley. Pollution from vehicular emission is high, although there is a restriction on import of vehicles below Euro III standard. Emission check is mandatory during annual vehicle registration renewal; however, the quality of test is questionable. Government subsidy on kerosene and diesel has been removed. Roughly 600,000 improved cooking stoves in rural areas help in reducing indoor air pollution; nevertheless, this is not sufficient. Industrial pollution, although less catastrophic, is inadequately monitored, and clean development mechanism is not

[55] Government of Nepal, Central Bureau of Statistics. 2012. *National Population and Housing Census 2011*. Kathmandu.
[56] Government of Nepal, National Planning Commission. 2013. *Millennium Development Goal Acceleration Framework. 2013*. Kathmandu.
[57] Government of Nepal. Central Bureau of Statistics. 2008. International Union for Conservation of Nature. September 2001. *Transport Sector Air Pollution Survey in Major Urban Cities and Towns*. Kathmandu.
[58] Government of Nepal, Ministry of Urban Development. 2017. *National Urban Development Strategy 2017*. Kathmandu.

properly promoted. Unplanned sprawl of urban areas lacking proper sewerage and solid waste management systems has critically polluted urban rivers due to direct sewage and solid waste disposal. Despite having sufficient legal base for safeguarding the environment, the government has not been able to effectively monitor and enforce the legal requirements due to insufficient political will, resources, and capacity.

G. Solid Waste Management

The rapidly changing consumption behavior has increased the rate of waste production—both in volume and type, particularly in urban areas. Around 800 to 1,000 tons of waste is produced daily in the Kathmandu Valley. A study conducted by ADB in 2013 in 58 municipalities found that the average municipal solid waste collection efficiency in Nepal was 62.2% and the disposal rate is merely 37%. The figures are bound to be dismal after establishing 293 municipalities, many of them having rural characteristics. In the absence of sanitary landfill site, the collected wastes are generally disposed in river, natural drainages or forest areas. The highest fraction of household waste composition was organic waste (66%), plastic (12%), and paper (9%).[59] Establishing the 3R (reduce, reuse, and recycle) mechanism could significantly ease the waste management problems. Composting organic waste, minimizing waste generation, and recycling can largely reduce the woes of waste management. Management of medical waste is also a challenge, with most of the hospitals and nursing homes disposing hazardous medical waste mixed with common solid waste. Only few hospitals have functional incinerators to safely burn their medical waste.

The Solid Waste Act 2011 and the Solid Waste Management Rules 2013 are the two key legal provisions in solid waste management. Both policies have made the municipalities responsible for the construction, operation, and management of infrastructure for collection, treatment, and final disposal of solid waste by following the 3R principle. The acts have

also provision for involving the private sector, community organizations, and nongovernment organizations in solid waste management. Although the private sector has been collecting waste from the households by imposing service charge, they dump the collected waste in transfer station or in the open public land. Since the government could not demonstrate an efficient and well-managed operation in existing sanitary landfill sites, communities oppose the construction of a landfill site near their settlement. Hence, public awareness is vital for effective waste management. A stringent enforcement of "polluters pay" mechanism may discourage and minimize unnecessary waste generation.

H. Transportation

The transport sector is guided by policies, standards, and master plans.[60] These policies recognize the need to strengthen connectivity and develop and extend a road network that brings all people within reach of an all-season road within four hours walk in the hills and mountains, and two hours walk in the Terai, but weakly address the need for climate and disaster proofing.[61] The road subsector is one of the highest priorities in the government's annual planning and budgeting.[62] Road constructions in rural villages have been prioritized to improve mobility in widely dispersed settlements. However, many rural roads are non-engineered roads constructed by local bodies to meet popular demand of local villagers. These non-engineered roads are constructed in fragile hill slopes and watersheds without environmental considerations. Hence, road construction is directly related with the increase in the likelihood of landslides,[63] erosion, watershed degradation, and dust nuisance. The strategic roads are engineered; however, they are mostly constructed without taking into account environmental degradation caused by poor quarry operation, spoil disposal, and drainage management—damaging forests and watersheds. The Nepal Road Standard 2017 does envisage cycle track, footpath, tree plantation, and noise barriers, but has made them conditional and generally overlooked. The "infrastructure first" mindset and overlooking the

---

[59] See footnote 10.
[60] National Transportation Policy 2002; Nepal Road Standard 2017; Nepal Road Safety Action Plan 2013 – 2020; Strategic Road Network Master Plan 2004–2024; Priority Investment Plan 2007–2016; National Transport Policy 2001; Local Infrastructure Development Policy 2004; Environmental and Social Management Framework 2007; Environmental Assessment of the Road Sector in Nepal 2000; Environmental Management Guidelines 1999.
[61] P. B. Rana and B. Karmacharya. 2014. *A Connectivity-Driven Development Strategy for Nepal: From a Landlocked to a Land-Linked State. ADBI Working Paper Series.* No. 498. Tokyo: Asian Development Bank Institute.
[62] ADB. 2013. *Risk Assessment and Risk Management Plan: Transport Sector-Nepal.* Linked Document to the Country Partnership Strategy 2013-2017. Manila.
[63] B. G. McAdoo et al. 2018. *Brief Communication: Roads and Landslides in Nepal: How Development Affects Risk.* https://doi.org/10.5194/nhess-2017-461.

importance of environmental safeguards by relevant agencies while developing roads have been the key hindrance in developing a sustainable and environment friendly transport system.

I. Industrial Development and Pollution Control

The industry sector began to emerge in Nepal only in the 1980s, consisting of mainly cottage and medium-scale industries without significant levels of pollution. Several industrial estates were set up to promote industrial development, which succeeded to some extent. As per the industrial census of FY2011/2012, there were about 4,076 manufacturing industries in Nepal. However, the average contribution of the industry sector to GDP diminished from 22% in 2000 to 15% in 2010, due to armed conflict, labor disputes, and energy crisis.

Industries in Nepal include service industry (tourism, hotels, and restaurants); carpets and textiles weaving and leather production; rice, jute, sugar, and oilseed processing; instant noodles and beverages; cigarettes; and cement, paint, brick and steel, and iron-allied industries. In the face of lax government monitoring, most of the industries openly dispose their waste—polluting air, water, and soil. Industries annually produce 8.6 million m^3 of wastewater; 9,592 tons of total suspended solids; and 21,900 tons of solid waste. The total suspended particulate matter discharged by industries was 76,250 tons, with brick kilns and cement industries contributing 70% and 27%, respectively.[64] Nevertheless, the industries were mostly small to medium size, and the pollution incurred by them still reversible.

J. Tourism

Tourism industry in Nepal is intricately linked to natural resources and its success depends on water, energy, wildlife, food, and landscapes management. Although tourism could have a significant negative impact on natural resources and the environment, it also contributes to the conservation through awareness, investment in natural resources, and income generation. Promotion of nature-based tourism is gaining popularity. The natural beauty, ancient world heritage sites, cultural diversity and the protected areas of Nepal are the major tourist attractions. National parks and wildlife reserves are the most visited places representing nature-based tourism.[65] Nature-based tourism therefore has the potential to generate employment and increase GDP.

The major constraints to tourism growth are lack of quality infrastructure and sanitary facilities, decline in the status and values of natural and cultural heritage, pressure on the environment, limited access to new tourism areas, and pollution.

The arrival of tourists in Nepal, which started in the early 1970s, introduced new and non-biodegradable materials such as plastic, cans, and fast food—transforming the very nature of solid waste in the country. Mountain tourism encouraged local people to open lodge and restaurants, which used firewood for cooking and heating, causing forest degradation. Mountaineering has also its own problems; in June 2019, a cleanup crew recovered about 11 tons of waste and 4 dead bodies from Mount Everest. Wastes were left behind by the mountaineers, despite regulation to bring these wastes back from the mountain. Although the introduction of eco-tourism and home-stay facilities has increased public awareness to conserve natural resources while attracting tourists, a significant shift in conservation approach is yet to be recognized.

K. Climate Change

Nepal contributes only 0.027% to the global greenhouse gas (GHG) emission, but is most vulnerable to the impacts of climate change.[66] Nepal's diverse topography, fragile ecosystems, poverty, lack of capacity to plan effectively for climate change adaptation, and weak governance have made the country extremely vulnerable to the impacts of climate change. Nepal ranked 4th out of 124 countries in Climate Risk Index and 11th out of 181 countries on average during 1998–2017, indicating that the country is the most climate-vulnerable in the world.[67] The shrinking glaciers, a three- to four-week shift in the monsoon, and extreme climatic events (droughts, sudden cloud-bursts followed by flash floods and landslides, extreme temperature during winter and summer) are a manifestation of the impacts of climate change.[68] The mean temperature of the country has increased at a linear rate of 0.04°C per year (higher than the mean global rate).[69] The Intergovernmental Panel on

64 Government of Nepal, Ministry of Science, Technology and Environment. 2009. *Industrial Environment Study.* Kathmandu.
65 Government of Nepal, Ministry of Culture, Tourism and Civil Aviation. 2019. *Nepal Tourism Statistics 2018.* Kathmandu.
66 Government of Nepal, Ministry of Population and Environment. 2016. *Intended Nationally Determined Contributions.* Kathmandu.
67 Government of Nepal, Ministry of Population and Environment et. al. 2016. *Nepal Earthquake 2015: A Socio-Demographic Impact Study.* Kathmandu.

Climate Change reports that in the future, it is probable that the country's temperature will increase and precipitation will be more unpredictable, causing floods, landslides, snow melt and GLOF, and droughts and forest fires. The report suggests that in order to counter the impacts of climate change, it is essential to draw implications from both types of disasters and pursue solutions at the local, regional, and national levels.[70]

Studies have indicated that climate change will alter Nepal's river flows resulting to more drought and food scarcity and the region will become more arid during non-monsoon seasons due to less snow melting in the Himalayas. Erratic weather patterns, unpredictable and intense rainfall, reduced snowfall at high altitudes, recurrent droughts and floods, and a shift in the temperature regime have adversely affected agriculture and livelihoods of the poor, marginalized, and vulnerable communities that are dependent on subsistence farming. The government estimates 1.9 million people are highly vulnerable, and an additional 10 million are increasingly at risk to potential climate change impacts. Water resources, food security, and ecosystem health have been identified as most at risk.[71] Climate change impacts are already felt through watershed degradation, drying up of water sources, droughts, forest fires, and water-induced disasters.[72] The economic cost of climate change in agriculture, hydropower, and water-induced disasters is estimated at 2%–3% of GDP per year by 2050.[73] Although, Nepal lacks the required level of knowledge and capacity to analyze climate indicators, make predictions on impending events, and develop resilience to risks.

To decrease the effects of climate change, the Government of Nepal has prepared its National and Local Adaptation Program of Action (NAPA and LAPA) with support from the United Nations Development Programme (UNDP)–Global Environment Facility; Department for International Development of the United Kingdom (DFID); and Danish International

Box III-2: Risk of GLOF in Nepal

Himalayan glaciers, in general, are shrinking and glacial lakes are evolving and growing rapidly in number and size as a result of climate change, thus increasing the risks of glacial lake outburst flood (GLOF). GLOF can be impounded by moraine complexes, glacial ice or even bedrock and, as a result of breaching, slope failure, overtopping or other failure mechanisms, lead to catastrophic phenomena in the high mountains that threaten people's lives, livelihoods and regional infrastructure. The frequency and risk from potential GLOFs are expected to increase as the climate continues to change. It is, therefore, important to assess the overall GLOF risk for better planning and implementation of disaster risk reduction and climate change adaptation.

Source: https://www.icimod.org/mountain/glacial-lake-outburst-flood/

Development Agency.[74] The document identifies different priority projects and recognizes the need for local-level adaptation plans (footnote 70). Although the government has initiated adaptation plans, its implementation has remained a challenge.

Box III-3: Climate Change

Climate-change-driven events, such as melting glaciers, pose a grave risk to Nepal's economy, and could cause losses equal to almost 2.2% of annual GDP by 2050 and 9.9% by 2100. However, if mitigation and adaptation steps are taken, the damage could be limited to around 2.4% of GDP by 2100.

Source: ADB. 2014. *Assessing the Cost of Climate Change and Adaptation in South Asia.* Manila.

68 Government of Nepal, Ministry of Science, Technology and Environment. 2010. *National Adaptation Programme of Action to Climate Change.* Kathmandu.
69 S. K. Baidya, S. K. Regmi, and M. L. Shrestha. 2007. *Observed Climate Change and Climate Variability in Nepal.* Kathmandu.
70 World Resources Institute. 2018. *Climate Change in Nepal: Impacts and Adaptive Strategies.* Wri.Org. http://www.wri.org/our-work/project/world-resources-report/climate-change-nepal-impacts-and-adaptive-strategies.
71 Government of Nepal, Ministry of Environment. n.d. Nepal: Strategic Program for Climate Resilience. Kathmandu.
72 ADB. 2013. Environment Assessment (Summary). Linked Document to the Country Partnership Strategy, Nepal 2013–2017. Manila; ADB. 2014. *Assessing the Costs of Climate Change and Adaptation in South Asia.* Manila.
73 ADB. 2016. *Asian Development Outlook 2016: Asia's Potential Growth.* Manila.
74 See footnote 70.

Climate change is predicted to lead into major changes in freshwater flows with dramatic impacts on biodiversity and on people and their livelihood. The most striking loss will be the availability of surface water for domestic use particularly in the hills and mountains, where people depend on rivulets and springs. The drying out of water sources due to the impacts of climate change has already led to the abandoning of entire villages in Mustang, Jajarkot, Udaypur and Siraha districts (Kathmandu Post 7 November 2016).

L. Disaster Risk

The fragile and "young" geology of the Himalaya, unstable slopes, high topographical variation, low-lying areas in plains, extreme climatic events, environmental degradation, urbanization, unsustainable infrastructure development, and the country's modest socioeconomic conditions have made Nepal one of the most vulnerable countries in the world to natural hazards. The country is vulnerable to various forms of natural hazards including floods, landslides, flash floods, droughts, cold waves and heat waves, thunderstorms, fires, avalanches, and earthquakes. The biggest recorded disasters are the floods of 1993, 2008, and 2012; the earthquakes of 1934, 1988, and 2015; and the landslides of 1993 and 2014. Between 1980 and 2017, disasters in Nepal caused 21,000 deaths, affected the livelihoods of almost 13 million people, and resulted to approximately $12.6 billion in direct physical loss.[75] The 2015 Nepal Earthquake caused a loss of around 8,000 lives and damaged property estimated at $7.1 billion (equivalent to 35.7% of Nepal's 2014 GDP).[76] The 100-year probable maximum loss from earthquake is estimated at $1.4 billion.[77] Nepal ranked 11th in the world in terms of vulnerability to earthquakes and 30th in terms of flood risk.[78]

The lowlands of the Terai are prone to floods due to riverbank cutting and aggradation of riverbeds that expose settlements and agricultural land. Similarly, hilly areas are at risk of landslides due to the disturbance of fragile geological settings by human activities. The High Himalaya is vulnerable to the risks of avalanches and GLOFs, while wind erosion and desertification are common in the Trans-Himalayan region. There are 1,466 glacial lakes in Nepal, of which 21 are at high risk of GLOFs.[79] At least 14 GLOF events were recorded in the past indicating potential high risk in future. Settlements and infrastructures are both at risk of GLOF. Nine districts in the Terai were identified as the most vulnerable to flooding; 29 districts in the hills and mountains are vulnerable to landslides; and 22 districts in the Terai, hills, and mountains are vulnerable to drought.[80] Overall, about 2.2% of the country's total land area (0.6 million ha) has become uncultivable due to flooding or soil erosion, up from 1.2% in 2001 (0.3 million ha). The Kathmandu Valley, due to its substandard and non-engineered buildings and unplanned and highly dense settlement, is the most at risk city in the world to earthquakes.[81]

Despite all odds, Nepal initiated some positive gains in disaster risk management. In 2017, the Disaster Risk Reduction and Management Act was passed,[82] and the National Disaster Risk Reduction Policy and Strategic Action Plan 2017–2030 (NDRRPSAP) was finalized.[83] The Nepal Earthquake Post Disaster Recovery Framework 2016–2020 was approved in 2016.[84] The National Disaster Risk Reduction Policy and Strategic Action Plan proposes strategic actions for (i) developing legal frameworks, (ii) interagency coordination, (iii) developing early warning systems, (iv) capacity building

---

[75] See footnote 28.
[76] See footnote 73.
[77] UN. 2015. Global Assessment Report 2015. New York. http://www.preventionweb.net/english/hyogo/gar/2015/en/profiles/GAR_Profile_NPL.pdf.
[78] UNDP. 2004. A Global Report: Reducing Disaster Risk. New York.
[79] See footnote 50.
[80] Government of Nepal, Ministry of Science, Technology and Environment. 2010. National Adaptation Program of Action (NAPA) to Climate Change. Kathmandu.
[81] Geohazard International. 2016. Kathmandu Valley Earthquake Risk Management. California.
[82] Government of Nepal. 2017. Disaster Risk Reduction and Management Act 2017. Kathmandu.
[83] Government of Nepal, Ministry of Home Affairs. 2017. National Strategic Action Plan for Disaster Risk Reduction 2017–2030. Kathmandu.
[84] Government of Nepal, National Reconstruction Authority. 2016. Nepal Earthquake 2015 Post Disaster Recovery Framework 2016–2020. Kathmandu.

and institutional strengthening, and (v) promoting community based disaster risk management, among others. Nepal has started the establishment of a national disaster management authority, as suggested by National Disaster Risk Reduction Policy and Strategic Action Plan. Nepal is a signatory to Sendai Framework (2015–2030) for Disaster Risk Reduction, The United Nations Office for Disaster Risk Reduction and has been complying with its commitments. Disaster risk management in Nepal is primarily constrained by the lack of database for risk assessment to operationalize disaster information management system, local level disaster risk management plan and capacity, and human resource and logistical facilities to combat disaster events. The country's vulnerability is exacerbated by weak planning and coordination; rudimentary early warning systems; inefficient preparedness for disaster risks; and inadequate relief, recovery, and reconstruction capacity.

IV. INSTITUTIONAL ARRANGEMENT FOR ENVIRONMENTAL SAFEGUARDS

A. Legislative and Policy Framework

The Constitution of Nepal, Article 30, articulates the citizens' right to live in a clean and healthy environment and the rights and responsibilities of all levels of governance to enhance environment friendly development. Article 51 of the Constitution focuses on the enhanced role of the private sector in formulating sustainable socioeconomic development strategies and programs for developing environment friendly sustainable physical infrastructures with a regional balance. The policies also focus on generating and developing renewable energy to ensure reliable supply of energy. The policies emphasize that the negative impacts of industrialization and physical development will be mitigated through public awareness on environmental cleanliness. As a constitutional body, the National Natural Resources and Fiscal Commission mandated the government agencies to prepare recommendations to protect the environment through pollution control. There are several sector laws relevant to inclusive green growth (IGG) specific to transportation, energy, and urban services, and to the roles of specific agencies.

The Environment Protection Council, the Climate Change Council, the Parliamentary Committee for Natural Resource Management and Environment, and the Ministry of Forest and Environment (MOFE) are the apex agencies responsible for formulating national environment policies, programs, and regulatory frameworks for safeguards enforcement. The provincial government addresses forest and environment protection through their dedicated ministry. The environmental safeguards procedure is guided by the National Environmental Policy and Action Plan 1993, Environment Protection Act 2019, and Environment Protection Regulation 1997 (amended from time to time). The Forest Act 1993, Forest Regulation 1995, National Park and Wildlife Protection Act 1973, and Regulation 1974 guide and enforce forestry and wildlife conservation. Nepal has also signed international commitments and is a party to a large number of international conventions. These institutional arrangements and legal documents have made prior environmental assessment (i.e., environmental impact assessment, initial environmental examination) and government approval mandatory for all infrastructure and development projects. Some of the major infrastructure and service sector agencies, including forest, energy, health, irrigation, and roads have prepared sectors safeguards policies and guidelines, and safeguard sections in their organization as formal or informal units. The policies, acts, regulations, and guidelines provide sufficient legal basis and authority for the government to enforce environmental safeguards in development activities. Nevertheless, the environment sector faces critical challenges in terms of governance. The quality of environmental assessment has improved but their implementation, monitoring, and enforcement require considerable improvement. The government is yet to utilize the environment assurance tools, such as the strategic environmental assessment (SEA), while formulating national and sector policies and programs. Although the new environment protection act 2019 has kept a provision of conducting SEA. Coordination among inter-sector government agencies and the capacity of enforcement agencies are weak. The Central Bureau of Statistics publishes annual environmental statistics of Nepal, which generally lacks annually updated data.

The federal governance system has given authority to local bodies to implement certain size of development infrastructure projects. They can raise tax for use of natural resources such as extraction of riverbed aggregates and a resourceful and capable forest products. However, these local bodies do not have environmental and social safeguards section to ensure that the natural resources are sustainably used and the development works are carried out in full compliance with environmental requirements.

The present institutional arrangement is devoid of subject-matter specialists and sufficient staff and resources. This has constrained their environmental monitoring and enforcement capacity. Local bodies issuing license for extraction of natural resources in order to raise tax may cause innumerable and irreversible environmental damages due to weak enforcement and contractors over-extracting the natural resources. The new environment protection act needs harmonization and regulation needs to be updated to adjust with the new federal governance system. Other policies, acts, and regulations to be formulated at the provincial and local levels should be harmonized with national laws, and comply with Nepal's commitments to international conventions, treaties, and protocols.

B. Institutional Arrangement

Nepal has entered into federal governance system with three levels of government at federal, provincial, and local levels based on the principles of cooperation, co-existence, and coordination. Sub-article (8) of the Constitution states that the Federal Parliament may make laws with respect to matters enumerated in Schedule (6), which also lists use of forests, water resources, and management of environment.

The Ministry of Environment (MOE) was established in 1995 with the responsibility for environmental conservation, pollution control, conservation of national heritage, and preparation of national legislation on environmental protection. The ministry went through several reorganizations, and now named as the Ministry of Forest and Environment (MOFE). With such frequent changes in institutional arrangements, the ministry faced difficulties in proper institutionalization, monitoring, and enforcement of safeguards compliance activities. MOFE also functions as the secretariat of the Climate Change Council and the Environment Protection Council; however, both councils have been inactive. The Department of Environment under MOFE looks after monitoring and enforcement of environmental regulations, but it lacks sufficient staffing. The five sections of the department on climate change, environmental standards, environmental assessment, sustainable development and adaptation, and clean development mechanism have altogether 16 technical staff. The department does not have decentralized offices, limiting their outreach in the subnational level.

MOFE has virtually no vertical links with provincial and local governments, which restricts the implementation of environmental policies and enforcement at all levels of governance. This has rendered confusion on sharing of natural resources and payment for environmental services. In practice, the responsibility for environmental management and capacity at local levels is close to non-existent. Interagency coordination in environment management is comparatively weak, and there is no national environmental monitoring network and database. Given the inadequate human resources, technical capacity, and funds, MOFE finds it extremely difficult to carry out effective and efficient environmental monitoring and management. MOFE has not been able to adopt important strategy and policy documents—which are still at the draft stage.

The current governance structure gave space for establishing environment focal sections in most of the government ministries and departments at federal and provincial levels. Local bodies also have environment section, although mostly defunct in the absence of staff and resources. The environment sections in federal ministries are either formal or informal, and they look after sector-related safeguard issues. Most of these sections are constrained with limited staff, resources, and capacity to address environmental and climate change risks. Authority to approve initial environmental examinations (IEEs) lies with the concerned federal ministries, whereas MOFE has the authority to approve EIA.

The Ministry of Home Affairs is the focal ministry for managing disaster risks. The Ministry of Agriculture and Livestock Development is responsible for minimizing environmental risks from farming practices, conserving biodiversity, and mitigating the impacts of climate change. The Nepal Army protects the national parks. Chief wardens in the national parks are appointed by MOFE, who have the power to take legal action against poachers or encroachers, or anyone who harasses or injures wildlife. As a result, the national parks are well-protected and wildlife population has been gradually increasing. Besides government agencies, there are more than 1,300 nongovernment organizations (NGOs), civil society organizations, research institutions, academic institutions, laboratories, and media organizations that work on and advocate for environmental conservation. The National Trust for Nature Conservation supports the government in managing conservation areas. Agencies such as WWF and International Union for Conservation of Nature Nepal also support biodiversity conservation. The Ministry of Urban Development is responsible for planned and sustainable management of urban environment. Transportation management and vehicular emissions are monitored by the Department of Transport, and pollution by industries is monitored by the Department of Industry and the Department of Environment. The Ministry of Energy, the Department of Electricity Development, and the Nepal Electricity Authority (NEA) are responsible for managing the energy sector. Scores of environmental assessment and management guidelines for the energy sector have been prepared. NEA has a specialized environment and social studies department, to ensure safeguards in the energy development projects implemented by the government or the private sector.

In 2007, the government constituted a climate change network under the chairpersonship of the Secretary of the then MOSTE, now MOFE, to coordinate stakeholders. The Climate Change Council was constituted on 23 July 2009 under the Prime Minister's chairpersonship to provide guidance on the formulation and implementation of climate change policies, plans, and programs, and take the lead in climate change international negotiations. Nepal is actively participating in the least developed countries' climate change coordination group of the United Nations Framework Convention on Climate Change.

The government has taken several initiatives to promote adaptation to climate-change- and climate-resilient development, and has prepared climate change policy and national and local adaptation plan of action. The government regularly participates in the UNFCCC-organized annual conference of parties (COP) on climate change, which demonstrates the importance given to partnering for climate change mitigation and adaptation plan of action.

C. Safeguard Capacity of Federal Government Agencies

ADB's Nepal Resident Mission conducted an assessment of the safeguards capacity of 24 federal government agencies (ministries and departments) in 2019.[85] The Department of Environment, the Environment and Social Studies Department of the Nepal Electricity Authority, the Ministry of Forest and Environment (MOFE), and the Department of Electricity Development have all scored more than 80% in a scale of 100% on environmental safeguards performance due to their better institutional capacity, staffing, and resources in safeguards implementation. The MOFE and its Department of Environment are the focal government agencies of Nepal responsible for overall national level plan and policy preparation and enforcement. The environmental safeguard capacity of more than 50% central government agencies implementing environment sensitive larger infrastructure was found to be just satisfactory. They have informal environment/safeguard unit which are semi-functional or nonfunctional in the absence of sufficient staff and budget. Some of these government agencies belong to the urban development, rural infrastructure and irrigation subsector. A few of the larger infrastructure development agencies, such as the ADB Project Directorate/Department of Roads, the Civil Aviation Authority of Nepal, the Nepal Reconstruction Authority, the Kathmandu Upatyaka Khanepani Limited, and the High Powered Committee for Integrated Development of the Bagmati Civilization are yet to institutionalize a proper safeguard section with staff and resources. A major risk in pursuing sustainable development agenda lies on the fact that a certain scale of infrastructure development authority has been given to the local bodies (municipalities and rural municipalities) under the federal governance system. These agencies do not have proper institutional arrangement, staff with required capacity and resources to plan, monitor and enforce safeguards in their operation.

---

[85]   D.B. Singh. 2019. *Annual Environmental Compliance Monitoring Report 2019*. Kathmandu: ADB Nepal Resident Mission.

D. Legal and Regulatory Gaps

a. Major institutional gaps in environmental safeguards management

Inconsistencies and contradictions between sector plans and policies often weaken implementation mechanism and enforcement. Some of the issues in environmental safeguards management are discussed hereunder.

- Weak system of collecting and maintaining data and information;
- Activities implemented in isolation by sections/units of government agencies;
- Lack of systematic follow-up by MOFE on compliance with environmental management plan as agreed in EIA/IEE by the infrastructure developers (generally, field monitoring and enforcement are conducted only if there are serious complaints);
- Inefficient discharge of regulatory responsibilities by the government's environmental protection agency;
- Weak grievance handling and information dissemination mechanism;
- Overlapping mandates and duplication of work between and among divisions of the ministry and departments; and
- Confusion on institutional roles and responsibility, and lack of coordination between provincial and local governments.

b. Gaps in coordination between MOFE and provincial and local governments

The interagency coordination between MOFE and sector ministries in the center has remained weak. There are gaps in mechanism to coordinate institutional roles and performance among agencies except during review and approval of EIA. The role of formulation of development plans and policies, including the incorporation of environmental management issues, lies with the National Planning Commission (NPC). However, the role of NPC in environmental management is limited and there is less meaningful coordination between NPC and MOFE on environmental matters. The Environment Protection Council, with MOFE as member secretary, was formed to serve the national environmental coordination function but has remained largely non-functional. As environmental management issues grow in significance and complexity, the need for interagency and intergovernmental coordination will be increasingly important. In this regard, MOFE could take the lead role in coordinating the environmental activities with various ministries, provinces, and local bodies.

The federal ministry barely has linkage with the provincial and local governments, and the mechanism of sharing safeguards assurance in their operations is yet to be established. Any coordination has been a "learning-by-doing" process. The provincial and local governments have environment sections, but they are almost non-functional. The sections in metropolis or sub-metropolis exist with some staff whose key responsibility is to manage municipal solid waste.

V. MAINSTREAMING INCLUSIVE GREEN GROWTH

A. The Green Growth

The World Bank defines inclusive green growth is to become "efficient in its use of natural resources, clean in that it minimizes pollution and environmental impacts, and resilient in that it accounts for climate change risks and natural hazards, and the role of environmental management and natural capital in preventing disasters and reducing poverty." The United Nations Environment Programme has defined green economy as resulting in "improved human well-being and social equity, while significantly reducing environmental risks and ecological scarcities." The Outcomes document of the United Nations Conference on Sustainable Development states that the green economy should contribute to eradicating poverty and sustained economic growth, enhancing social inclusion, improving human welfare, and creating opportunities for employment and decent work for all, while maintaining the healthy functioning of the earth's ecosystems. The Organisation for Economic Co-operation and Development defines green growth as the process of fostering economic growth and development, while ensuring that natural assets continue to provide the resources and environmental services on which our well-being relies upon.

Green growth has great potential to provide a clear and focused policy agenda to pursue sustainable economic growth, while improving resilience to climate change and other shocks, and preventing environmental degradation, biodiversity loss, and unsustainable natural resource use. A green growth paradigm supports development that is for more efficient in the use of natural resources– offering a win-win scenario for both environmental and economic dimension.[86] Green growth based on green economy is one of the alternatives to sustainable development. The unsustainable use of natural resources affects the global environmental trajectory on population and climate change, and on the increasing risks of food shortages.[87]

Hence, the country's transition to a greener development path is imperative.

Green growth is not a replacement of sustainable development, but an approach through which the aim of sustainable development could be achieved. Sustainability involves the conservation of natural capital for sustainable economic production and inter-generational equity. The ecological perspective of sustainability also requires that the integrity of ecosystems and diversity of species must be maintained.

ADB prepared its Environmental Operational Directions 2013–2020 to promote transitions to green growth in Asia and the Pacific. The new ADB Strategy 2030, which has the mission of prosperous, inclusive, resilient, and sustainable Asia and the Pacific, focuses on seven key operational priorities—one of them is "tackling climate

Box V-1: Growing Environmental Pressure

The key environmental issues facing the region include air pollution, water pollution inadequate waste management, deforestation, land degradation, and biodiversity loss. Growing environmental pressures pose challenges to sustainability and exacerbate existing vulnerabilities of the poor, who depend disproportionately on ecosystem services for their livelihoods and food security. The region also faces water scarcity because of the changes in climate as well as the increasing demand for water from the rapidly growing population and industrialization. Hence, resource conservation through the use of new technologies and effective implementation of public policies are crucial.

ADB. 2008. *Strategy 2020: The Long-Term Strategic Framework of the Asian Development Bank 2008–2020.* Manila.

---

[86] ADB. 2013. *Environment Operational Directions 2013-2020: Promoting Transition to Green Growth in Asia and the Pacific.* Manila.
[87] OECD. 2012. *Greening Development: Enhancing Capacity for Environmental Management and Governance.* Paris.

change, building climate and disaster resilience, and enhancing environmental sustainability."

To promote transition to green growth, and address the causes and consequences of climate change and disasters, four mutually supportive environment operational directions were identified:

(i) *Promote a shift to sustainable infrastructure.* Help developing member countries build infrastructure that contributes to environmentally sustainable and low-carbon development, and to increased resilience to climate change and disaster;

(ii) *Invest in natural capital.* Help reverse the decline of natural capital to ensure environmental goods and services can sustain future economic growth and well-being, build climate resilience, and contribute to carbon sequestration.

(iii) *Strengthen environmental governance and management capacity.* Build sound environmental governance and management capacity to improve environmental and natural resource management and strengthen country systems and environmental safeguards; and

(iv) *Respond to the climate change imperative.* Promote climate change response actions—both adaptation and mitigation—that will cut across the first three directions and be fully integrated in each of the directions.

B. Inclusive Green Growth Analysis

Majority of the people living in Nepal are dependent on agriculture and forestry for their livelihood. These sectors have not contributed much to greenhouse gas (GHG) emissions. The industrial development in the country

Figure V-1: **The Four Components of Inclusive Green Growth Principle**

Source: Asian Development Bank. 2013. *Environment Operational Directions, 2013–2020: Promoting Transitions to Green Growth in Asia and the Pacific.* Manila.

has been almost basic, and GHG emissions thereof are minimal. That is not to say, however, that Nepal is free of environmental problems. Environmental degradation has been increasing; urban population is constantly on the rise and consequent urban environmental degradation is rising commensurately; and modern agriculture and unsustainable forestry management practices are adding to environmental woes. Given that the world is increasingly resorting to the path of green economy, Nepal needs to follow that to remain competitive in the world market by adopting green economic policies. Since Nepal is yet to enter the industrialization phase, it is relatively easier for the country to adopt greener approach to future industrialized development.[88]

C. Inclusive Green Growth Challenges

The following are the underlying trends and challenges to IGG initiatives:

- The newly formed three-layer federal government system in which local bodies are made responsible for implementing local development activities. These newly formed bodies lack environmental safeguards capacity with staff and budget.

- Nepal is one of the 10 least urbanized yet one of the top ten fastest urbanizing countries in the world. The urban population increased by 3.2% per year on average during 2000–2017, rising from 13.4% of the population to 19.7% as people moved to cities in search of opportunities.[89] With the establishment of 293 urban centers, 59.9% of the total population was living in urban areas in FY2018. The rising urban population has significantly increased pressure on urban environment. While the urban management is demanding services, the slow nature of municipal development has caused a deterioration of the quality of life in the city, with substandard roads, poor sewerage system and solid waste management, air and water pollution, and declining urban aesthetics. As the demand for urban services increase, the rural areas receive pressure to supply food and other consumable items to meet these demands, which has environmental ramifications. A report from the United Nations Advisory Committee of Local Authorities elaborates that the cities should focus on creating enabling environment through equal access to jobs, productive urban design, innovative financing,

88 D. Bhuju et al. 2018. *Nepal's Green Economy Initiative and Framework (Proposed).* Kathmandu.
89 World Bank. 2019. *Nepal Environment Sector Diagnostic: Path to Sustainable Growth under Federalism. A Country Environment Analysis.* Washington, DC.

productive informal economy, and rural–urban linkages.[90] However, the municipalities in Nepal are performing "business as usual". Hence, the unplanned urban development is the biggest challenge for IGG.

- Nepal received remittances worth NPRs699 billion during FY2016/2017 ranking fourth in the list of countries with large contribution of remittances to GDP.[91] A study shows that remittances in Nepal have reached 32% of GDP.[92] The capital flows from remittances are primarily used for migrating from rural to nearby towns. The families move to the city for education of children, better employment opportunity, security, and end up living in a substandard environment. Due to lack of planning and accelerated urbanization, people are living in undeveloped sites deprived of access to power, water, and sanitation services. The remittance income is also changing the consumption habit leading to generation of non-biodegradable waste in rural and urban areas. Countries with inefficient and unproductive cities tend to lag behind in achieving effective development.[93] The intensity and velocity of urbanization pose challenges in terms of expansion of squatter settlements and shantytowns, exacerbating the problems of urban congestion and unhealthy living environment for the urban poor.

- The government's white paper on energy development, declared on 9 May 2018, has a plan to develop 3,000 MW of hydropower in 3 years; 5,000 MW in 5 years; and 15,000 MW in the next 10 years. In a hurry to meet the target they have declared IEE as sufficient for hydropower projects that are up to 50-megawatt capacity, irrespective of their ecological footprint and significance of impact.[94] An ongoing trend is that the environmental safeguards are well considered in projects funded by development partners. However, safeguards are least complied to in projects implemented by the private sector or by the government. In the haste to generate power, compromises with high risks are made in environmental compliances. Also, unplanned placing of dams across the rivers has affected the aquatic biodiversity, pushing many species to the brink of extinction.

- The sufficiency of electricity and increased FDI could boost investment in polluting industries. These industries may not invest in pollution control by taking advantage of the weak government monitoring and enforcement.

- Stones and aggregates from riverbed or hill slopes are over-exploited, particularly in the fragile area of Chure hills and mid-hills, causing huge impact on river morphology; erosion and landslides; and loss of forest, wildlife habitat, and aquatic biodiversity. Heavy sedimentation causes aggradation of riverbed in the downstream, causing floods in Terai. Whereas, massive riverbed material extraction near infrastructure has caused water level going below intake of irrigation systems and many bridges collapsed due to foundation exposure.

- The absence of good public transport system has compelled people to opt for private vehicles, increasing their import and adding greenhouse gases. Automobile exhaust is the highest contributor to increased GHG emission.

- The non-engineered and excavator-constructed rural roads in fragile hills, without environmental and social safeguards consideration, have huge impact on the hill ecosystem. Deforestation, habitat fragmentation, erosion, and landslides caused by haphazard construction of rural roads have resulted in large-scale environmental degradation annually with loss of properties and human lives.

- The Nepal Road Standard 2017 and Rural Road Standard 1999 (revision 2015) encourages the design of non-motorized interventions such as cycle track, footpath, zebra crossings. They also include provision for tree plantation, wildlife corridors, and noise barrier. However, these are not mandatory requirements and are generally not followed.

- The changing pattern of improved agriculture depends on agrochemicals and the development of a variety of climate-resilient seeds. Rampant use of fertilizer and pesticides has caused irreversible ecological damages on soil, and terrestrial and aquatic ecosystem.

- The lack of updated data and prevailing practice of ad hoc planning without referring to baseline information has been one of the root causes of environmental degradation and a challenge to green growth.

- The practice of working in silo and single-sector approach is a challenge in identifying cumulative impacts.

90   United Nations Advisory Committee of Local Authorities. 2013. *Job Creation and Local Productivity*. Barcelona.
91   Government of Nepal, Ministry of Labor. UN Migration Agency, International Labour Organization, and Asia Foundation. 2016. *Labor Migration for Employment – A Status Report for Nepal: 2015/2016 – 2016/2017*. Nepal.
92   International Fund for Agriculture Development. 2017. *Sending Money Home Contributing to SDGs, One Family at a Time*. Rome.
93   IOSR. 2016. *Journal of Humanities and Social Science* 21 (1) (Version II).
94   Government of Nepal, Ministry of Forest and Environment. 2019. *Draft Environment Protection Regulation 2019*. Kathmandu.

VI. INTEGRATED DIAGNOSTIC OF ENVIRONMENT AND NATURAL RESOURCES

A. Integrated Approach to Studying the Causes of Environmental Issues

The information and data collected from secondary sources and through consultation with relevant stakeholders were analyzed to identify the root causes of the gaps in environment protection, climate change, and disaster risk management. Based on the findings, attempts were made to establish the link of prevailing state of economy, poverty, and development activities with environmental degradation. Also, an integrated "cause-effect-impact" analysis was carried out (Figure VI-1) overarching the sectors and identifying the causes leading to environmental degradation.

The areas of analysis included past efforts in safeguarding the environment in the context of green growth, developing mitigation measures for the impacts of climate change and disaster risks, and the applicability of relevant institutional arrangement and legal frameworks. The outcome was analyzed to recommend strategies for safeguarding the environment and managing climate change and disaster risks to achieve the objective of sustainable development.

The broad mitigation measures were reassessed in terms of ADB's directives for ensuring a shift toward inclusive green growth solutions. Based on these, recommendations were offered for mainstreaming environmentally sustainable development in ADB investments through the new CPS.

B. Records from Stakeholders Consultation on CIDENAR

The in-country capacity (in relation to environmental and social safeguards for IGG) is inadequate and requires effective knowledge sharing among and capacity building of the government, consultants, and contractors. The challenge in mainstreaming environment, climate change, and disaster risk management in planning, design, and implementation process has exponentially increased after formation of federal, provincial, and local governments—which have limited safeguards knowledge, capacity, and resources to plan and implement development works under sustainable development and IGG principles. In this regard, various experts and government agencies were consulted on the challenges in mainstreaming environmental protection and climate change risks in projects and programs, and in following the principles of inclusive green growth in overall country operation. The recommendations highlighted by the participants during the consultation are briefly discussed below:

- Make cumulative impact assessment and strategic environmental assessment (SEA) as part of national environment protection act (the new Environment Protection Act 2019 has considered provision of conducting SEA) and regulation.
- Encourage use of NAPA's climate vulnerability mapping for planning purposes.
- Establish coherency among projects to address issues on air quality, water, solid waste, nature conservation, and health.
- Develop projects to open up new markets by stimulating demand for green goods, services, and technologies.
- Ensure that projects follow environment friendly procedures and guidelines and comply with environmental clearances from government.
- Implement projects related to IGG education, awareness, and green skills development. Green and low carbon solutions in Nepal should create green jobs, help produce surplus green products for national and international markets, and enable producers to better

access regional and global markets. Promote public-private partnership to enhance greening of products through forward and backward linkages.

- Link projects for green economic opportunities to livelihood and environmental gains, such as community forestry, organic farming, ecotourism, forest-based livelihoods approach, and renewable energy solutions.
- Focus on the promotion of drought-resistant crop and water conserving technologies.
- Include and complement the government's environmentally conscious initiatives, such as eco-friendly rural roads. These have been indicative of the government's effort to strive for sustainable development. The Government of Nepal passed the Environmentally Friendly Local Governance framework as part of an umbrella public policy. ADB projects should include and complement such initiatives and frameworks. Simple technologies, use of local resources, participatory approach and environmental considerations are the important principles of green road concept.
- Implement climate change adaptation through implementation of National and Local Adaptation Program of Action (NAPA and LAPA).
- Promote green infrastructure investments.
- Enhance productivity by creating incentives for greater efficiency in the use of natural resources, reducing waste and energy consumption, and allocating resources to the highest value-added use.
- Support Nepal to combat climate change and disaster risks through accessing funds for investment in natural capital, strengthening capacity, and marketing of environmental services, such as carbon sequestration in international markets.

C. Provincial Stakeholders Consultation for CPS Preparation

Extensive consultations were carried out and suggestions were solicited from the provincial stakeholders including political parties, government staff, local NGO, community-based organization, media, and academia. The suggestions are listed below:

Province 2, Janakpur
- Place dam in Chure and irrigate the fertile lands in Terai by transferring water from water-sufficient basins to the water stressed areas.

- Conserve Chure, which is a priority of Province 2. Water sources are drying up and erosion and landslides in Chure are damaging agricultural lands in Terai. The fertile land of Terai will face desertification in 50 years if Chure is not conserved. Hence, protect Chure from encroachment, damage by unplanned infrastructure construction, and deforestation.
- Protect national forest and save trees while constructing big infrastructure.
- Implement quality projects and invest on environmental sustainability, good governance and adaptation to climate change risks.
- Generate 50-MW solar power in Province 2.
- Continue support for sustainable urban development in upcoming towns.
- Capacity development of provincial staff in sustainable development.

Gandaki Province, Pokhara
- Undertake lake conservation for tourism development.
- Establish solar power plants in Manang and Mustang districts.
- Ensure social inclusion in protecting the environment and in addressing climate change risks.
- Conserve and protect the Narayani River.

Bagmati Province, Hetauda
- Use forest resources scientifically for economic benefits.
- Give priority to forest and watershed conservation for sustainable development.
- Prioritize the protection and conservation of Chure to save Terai from desertification.
- Develop park in the bank of Narayani River in Bharatpur metropolis.
- Prioritize establishment of sanitary landfill sites in municipalities.

Province 5, Butwal
- Shift all polluting industries (cement) from 5-kilometer radius of Lumbini.
- Protect forests.
- Construct river training and flood protection in Tinau River.
- Implement project for urban environment improvement.

Figure VI-1: Integrated Cause and Effect Analysis and Recommended Inclusive Green Growth Measures

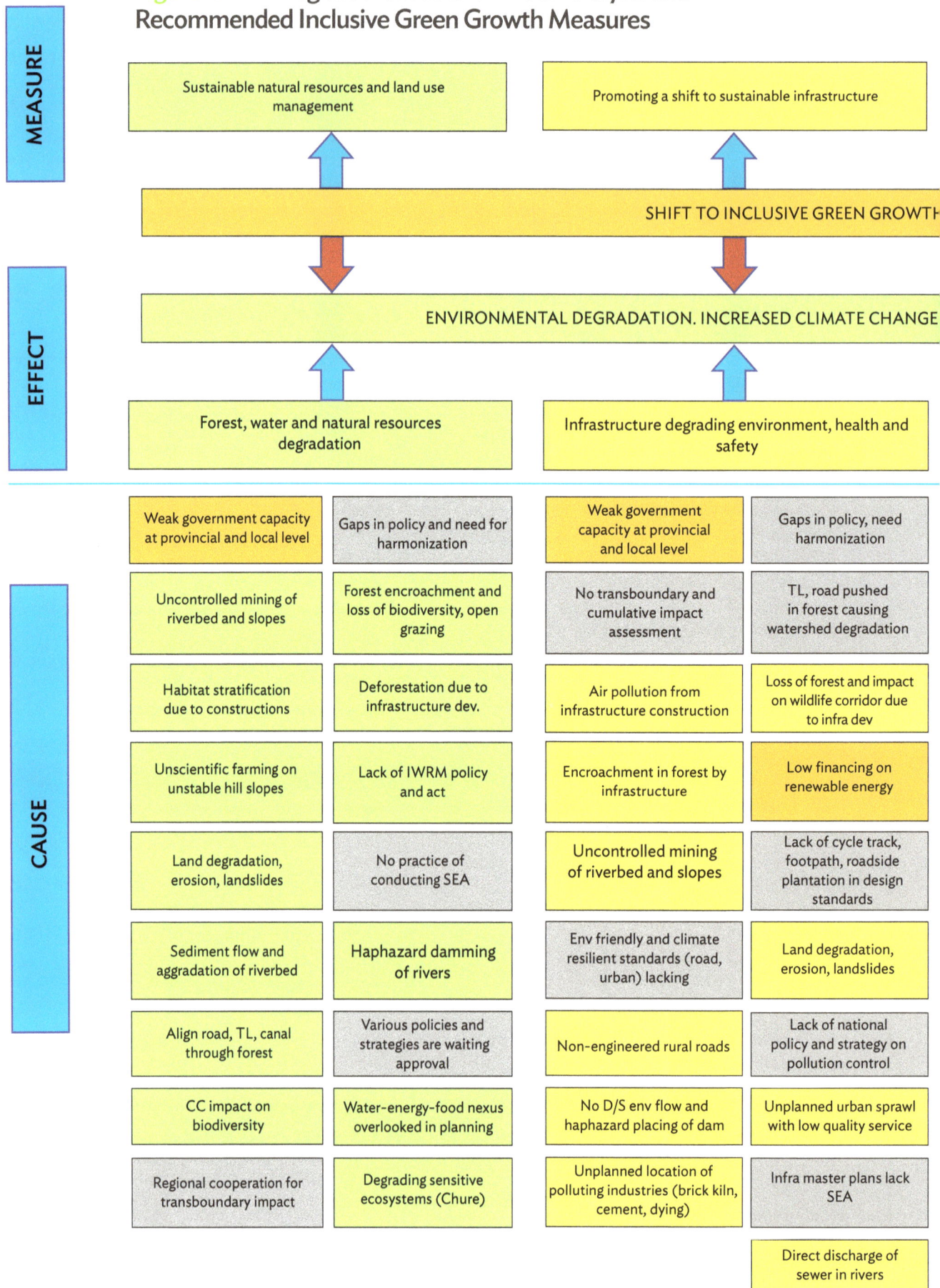

| MEASURE | Sustainable natural resources and land use management | Promoting a shift to sustainable infrastructure |

SHIFT TO INCLUSIVE GREEN GROWTH

ENVIRONMENTAL DEGRADATION. INCREASED CLIMATE CHANGE

| EFFECT | Forest, water and natural resources degradation | Infrastructure degrading environment, health and safety |

CAUSE

Weak government capacity at provincial and local level	Gaps in policy and need for harmonization	Weak government capacity at provincial and local level	Gaps in policy, need harmonization
Uncontrolled mining of riverbed and slopes	Forest encroachment and loss of biodiversity, open grazing	No transboundary and cumulative impact assessment	TL, road pushed in forest causing watershed degradation
Habitat stratification due to constructions	Deforestation due to infrastructure dev.	Air pollution from infrastructure construction	Loss of forest and impact on wildlife corridor due to infra dev
Unscientific farming on unstable hill slopes	Lack of IWRM policy and act	Encroachment in forest by infrastructure	Low financing on renewable energy
Land degradation, erosion, landslides	No practice of conducting SEA	Uncontrolled mining of riverbed and slopes	Lack of cycle track, footpath, roadside plantation in design standards
Sediment flow and aggradation of riverbed	Haphazard damming of rivers	Env friendly and climate resilient standards (road, urban) lacking	Land degradation, erosion, landslides
Align road, TL, canal through forest	Various policies and strategies are waiting approval	Non-engineered rural roads	Lack of national policy and strategy on pollution control
CC impact on biodiversity	Water-energy-food nexus overlooked in planning	No D/S env flow and haphazard placing of dam	Unplanned urban sprawl with low quality service
Regional cooperation for transboundary impact	Degrading sensitive ecosystems (Chure)	Unplanned location of polluting industries (brick kiln, cement, dying)	Infra master plans lack SEA
			Direct discharge of sewer in rivers

| Strengthening environmental governance and management capacity | Responding to climate change imperative |

RINCIPLE OF SUSTAINABLE DEVELOPMENT

ND DISASTER RISKS. DEEPENS THE VICIOUS CYCLE OF POVERTY

| Widespread environmental consequence from weak monitoring and enforcement | Critical socioeconomic impacts of climate change |

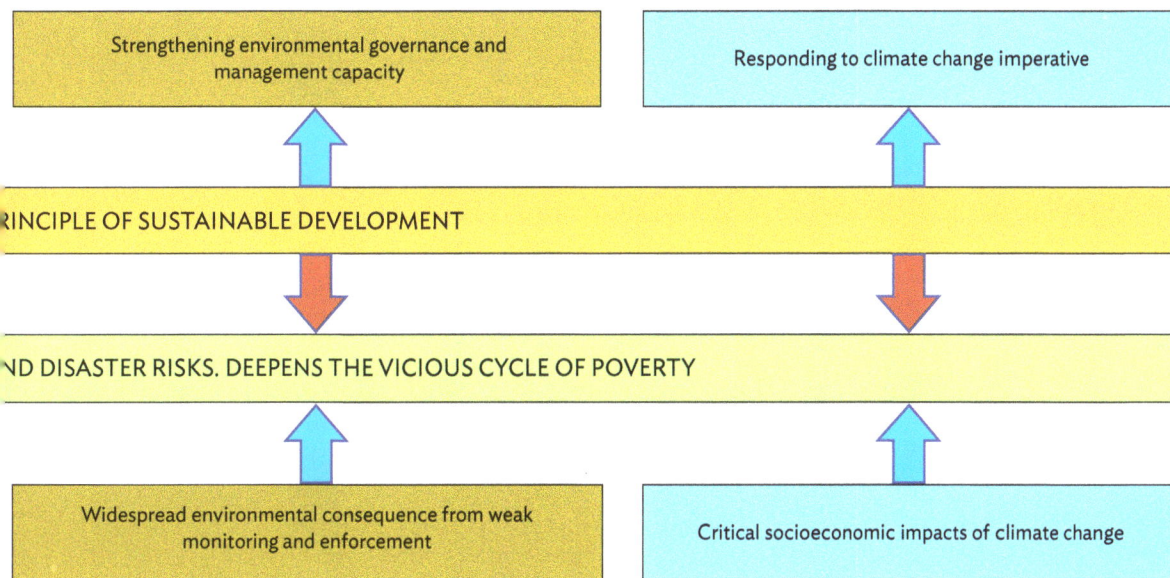

Weak government capacity, particularly at provincial and local levels	Gaps in policy, need harmonization. Many policies are at draft	Weak government capacity at all levels in climate change	Weak implementation of policy, NAPA, LAPA
Lack of environment friendly standards (road, urban)	Nepal weak in negotiation in international market for payment for environmental services	Extreme events (rainfall, flood, inundation, drought, drying of water sources)	Forest encroachment and loss of biodiversity also decreasing carbon sequestration
Old environment sector strategy and guidelines	Regional cooperation policy for transboundary impact	Indigenous and local knowledge in CC adaptation ignored	Increased GHG emission from use of fossil fuel and biomass
Monitoring and enforcement for environment protection weak	Unclear approach of government on issues (i.e., requirements of conservation area)	Low carbon economic development strategy in draft	Regional consultation for strategic partnership lacks for addressing climate change
Uncontrolled mining of aggregates and polluting industries not monitored	Uncontrolled env. damage by non-engineered, heavy machine constructed roads	Climate change risks not mainstreamed in infrastructure design standards	Lack of information, database, and scientific monitoring of climatic data and consequences
Lack of knowledge on climate resilient design	SEA is lacking for policy, strategy and masterplans	Rural area devoid of electricity and dependent on use of biomass (firewood, dung) causing deforestation	Declining productivity, drying water sources and impact on food security
Decreasing urban greenery and open space, room to play	Polluters pay principle not enforced		
	Poor SWM and lack of Reduce-Reuse-Recycle in solid waste management		

Source: CIDENAR Study Team, 2019
Note: CC= climate change, D/S= downstream, GHG=green house gas, IWRM=integrated water resource management, LAPA= local adaptation plan of action, NAPA= national adaptation plan of action, SEA=strategic environmental assessment, SWM=solid waste management, TL=transmission line.

D. Findings from Integrated Cause-Effect Analysis

The trend of FDI does not show much progress in Nepal. The existing investments are primarily in the service sector, and a few in cement and hydropower industry. The trend is not expected to suddenly rise to an environmentally threatening level, such as a surge in carbon emission or highly toxic industrial chemical pollution. The trend of industrial development is almost stagnant with few industries operating in food processing, beverage, dairy, cement, steel reinforcement and iron sheet manufacturing. Other industries are mostly small cottage type handicraft, garment, carpet, and pashmina. Hence, the environmental threat to Nepal is more attributed to environmentally damaging human-induced activities and transboundary causes (climate change and damming of rivers).

The study followed a cause-effect analysis by listing the causes and finding inter-linkages between them. The common causes and impacts were grouped together suggesting common recommendations. The causes of sector-specific impacts were further disaggregated and measures to mitigate the impacts were identified. Issues have been clustered following the guidance given by ADB's environmental operational directives for IGG 2013–2020. These clusters include sustainable infrastructure development, investment in natural capital, improving environmental governance, and climate change and disaster risk management. Each of the clusters was further analyzed, and recommendations were suggested. These are presented in the following sections.

VII. ENVIRONMENTAL DIRECTIVES FOR COUNTRY OPERATION TOWARD ACHIEVING INCLUSIVE GREEN GROWTH

A. Shift to Sustainable Infrastructure

There are at least three reasons to consider infrastructure as a strategic point of entry for green economy and productive employment in Nepal. First, infrastructure is critical for investment and growth in economic sectors. Lack of or poor quality infrastructure not only retards economic growth but also isolates and even discriminates against poorer communities living in remote areas. Second, infrastructure is a major sector of the economy. According to a World Bank study, infrastructure accounts for 3% to 8% of GDP in Nepal. The huge unskilled human resource, which migrates to other countries in search of job, could be utilized within the country through increasing employment opportunity by upscaling the size of infrastructure construction. Third, there are viable technological options that are considered green, which can be adopted, yet without the need to compromise on efficiency and productivity.[95]

ADB is committed to achieving a prosperous, inclusive, resilient, and sustainable Asia and the Pacific, while sustaining its efforts to eradicate extreme poverty. ADB will support in developing green and climate-friendly infrastructure projects that will contribute to fighting climate change, improving the quality of air and water, and reducing environmental degradation across the region.

The shift to sustainable infrastructure calls for environmentally sustainable, low-carbon, and climate-resilient infrastructure, including redesign, rehabilitation, reuse, or optimization of existing infrastructure.
Theme 1: Sustainable Transport
Theme 2: Clean Energy
Theme 3: Sustainable Urban Services

---

[95] See footnote 86.

Table VII-1-A: Sustainable Transport

Broad outline of sustainable transport component	<ul><li>Make transport system accessible, safe, environment friendly, and affordable as mentioned in ADB's Sustainable Transport Initiatives Operational Plan 2010.</li><li>Follow the approach of:<ul><li>– Avoid: reduce the need to travel such as cut unnecessary trips, join delinked connectivity, and encourage subregional transport.</li><li>– Shift: change to energy efficient mode, such as train, waterways, and bicycle.</li><li>– Improve: less polluting and energy efficient technologies, such as electric vehicles.</li></ul></li><li>Build on growing knowledge on pollution and GHG emissions by the transport sector.</li><li>Make transport sector investment environment friendly and minimize GHG emissions.</li><li>Minimize air pollution, spoilage, and noise.</li><li>Promote green technology.</li></ul>
Issues of concern while assessing inclusive green growth for sustainable transport	<ul><li>Federal governance structure has given authority to implement development projects to local bodies that do not have safeguard capacity, staff, and resources. This has increased the risk of managing environmental protection while implementing development activities.</li><li>Crusher plants for infrastructure construction operate under the license given by local administration. The crusher plant operators take advantage of weak government monitoring and enforcement, and over extract aggregate from riverbeds and fragile hill slopes much beyond the sustainable quantity, thus damaging the riparian ecosystem causing riverbed aggradation, degradation, flood, landslides, and loss of forest and wildlife habitats.</li><li>Nepal Road Standard 2014 (NRS) provides guidance for roadside tree plantation, environmental protection, and bioengineering, and promotes the use of non-motorized transportation; however, all these are not mandatory and are not generally followed.</li><li>Traditional bridge and suspension bridge building practices are effective climate-resilient technologies and provide vital link to rural areas in the event of disasters.</li><li>Wildlife crossings in roads passing from their movement corridors are rarely constructed in the absence of data and to minimize road construction cost.</li><li>Cycle track and footpath (more than 1.5 meters in width) are suggested in the NRS but is generally not followed.</li><li>Increasing import of vehicles and limited traffic management is affecting mobility and increasing pollution in the urban areas.</li><li>Non-engineered rural road constructions along the fragile hill slopes have caused disaster to environment with huge landslides, erosion, deforestation, and stratification of wildlife habitat. Poor maintenance and operation of heavy vehicles and tractors during monsoon has been the major reason for damage of road beyond operation, and loss of huge capital investments in construction and maintenance.</li><li>Air pollution has caused more than 1,600 premature deaths annually (MoPE 2005). Older vehicles, poor fuel quality, and wrong construction practices are some of the causes of air pollution.</li><li>Road traffic growth has led to increased traffic safety risks for pedestrians and cyclists.</li><li>Sound barriers in sensitive areas (settlement, religious areas, schools, and hospitals) are almost never considered in project design due little safeguard consciousness among designers and decision-makers.</li><li>Sustainable transport strategy states that sustainable transport system is achieved through integration of physical infrastructures (land use and transport), and coordination between various modes and networks. However, Nepal generally lacks the capacity and initiatives in all these areas.</li></ul>
Relevant action by ADB, Development Partners and Government*	<ul><li>About half a dozen strategic, rural roads and international airports are being implemented with ADB support. Environmental safeguards are integrated in project design.</li><li>Rural reconstruction and rehabilitation sector development project of Department for International Development of the United Kingdom (DFID- 2009–2013).</li><li>Rural Access Program (RAP) of DFID.</li><li>Project for strengthening the national rural transport program, World Bank.</li><li>Guidelines for District Transport Master Plan (DTMP) and use of existing plan prepared by government.</li><li>National Sustainable Transport Strategy (NSTS) for Nepal (2015–2040) from UN Center for Regional Development (UNCRD) support.</li><li>Road Safety Support Project, World Bank.</li></ul>

Recommendations for attaining IGG goal in sustainable transport	• Support in establishing safeguard sections in the sector offices with subject matter experts and sufficient budget (Project Implementation Directorate/Department of Roads, Project Management Directorate/Nepal Electricity Authority, Civil Aviation Authority of Nepal, Department of Local Infrastructure. • Institutional strengthening and capacity building of federal, provincial, and local government on environment-friendly development. • Follow the guidelines stated in ADB's Sustainable Transport Initiatives: Operational Plan 2010. • Update Nepal Road Standard, policy, and strategy by considering international best practices to shift toward sustainable transport. • Support in climate change considerations through shifting traffic into modes that have lower carbon emissions and through mainstreaming climate change in transport operations. • Encourage non-motorized transport infrastructure together with pedestrian zones and walkways, segregated cycle paths, and bicycle parking. Introduce improvement of standards for vehicle energy efficiency. • Prepare national, environmental, and natural resource database and operationalize national environmental management information system for informed decisions. • Conduct strategic environmental assessment (SEA) of the transportation sector policy and master plan. • Keep cost for environmental management plan (EMP) in bill of quantity (BOQ) and compliance provisions in contract agreement
ADB's comparative advantage	• ADB's existing in-house expertise and region-wide experience. • Established competence in transportation and close working relationship with executing agencies place ADB in a position to contribute meaningfully. • Proper operational policy through Sustainable Transport Initiative Operation Plan • and knowledge on best practices. • Good record of attracting cofinancing. • Ability to move faster than competitors. • Capacity to attract climate finance.

Sources: ADB. 2010. *Sustainable Transport Initiatives Operational Plan 2010*. Manila.

Note: * This is not an exhaustive list.

Table VII-1-B: Clean Energy

Sustainable energy means clean and renewable sources of energy—sources that renew themselves and will never get used up or depleted. It is inexhaustible and no GHG or pollution is emitted.

Broad outline of the sustainable energy component	• Support reliable, adequate, and affordable energy for social, economic, and environmental sustainability. • Broaden access to clean energy for all and replace biomass and fossil fuel-based consumption with renewable energy. • Build knowledge on pollution and GHG emissions by non-renewable and fossil fuel-based energy, and how renewable energy can replace that. • Promote energy-efficient green technology. • Act on the action plan suggested by ADB's Nepal Energy Sector Assessment, Strategy and Roadmap 2017. • Strengthen environmental safeguards by being more environmentally accountable. • Promote energy sector reform, capacity building, and good governance.
Issues of concern while assessing IGG for sustainable energy	• The federal governance structure has given authority to implement development projects to local bodies that do not have a safeguard capacity, staff, and resources. This has tremendously increased the risk of overlooking environmental protection while implementing projects. • Government white paper suggests rapid development in energy generation: 3,000 MW in 3 years; 5,000 MW in 5 years; and 15,000 MW of electricity in the next 10 years. Pursuing such high targets may compromise safeguard requirements. • The energy sector lacks a strategic environment assessment (SEA), without which, cumulative impacts could not be predicted and mitigation measures could not be prepared. • In the absence of knowledge on lifecycle movement of important fish species, hydropower developers are placing dams anywhere on rivers causing blockage to fish movement resulting in significant reduction of fish population. • Develop high-voltage transmission lines with regional power sharing perspective. • Avoid stratification of forest due to multiple transmission lines by developing one corridor across Chure and important forest areas. • Release a minimum 10% of the average of minimum river flow for sustaining the downstream aquatic ecosystem (Hydropower Policy 2001)—this is rarely complied.

Relevant action by ADB, Development Partners and Government*	• Energy access and efficiency improvement project, ADB.
	• 140 MW reservoir type Tanahu hydropower project, ADB.
	• More reservoir and run-of-the river systems are being designed by ADB with Dudhkoshi HEP in the 2020 pipeline.
	• Power transmission and distribution efficiency enhancement project (Phases I and II), ADB.
	• Electricity transmission expansion and supply improvement project, ADB.
	• Nepal's largest solar wind hybrid energy generation system (87 kWh per day) in Hariharpurgadhi, Sindhuli is under operation, ADB.
	• ADB Energy Policy 2009.
	• National act and regulation making IEE/EIA requirements mandatory.
	• Manuals in hydropower sector developed by Department of Electricity Development (DoED), Government of Nepal.
	• White paper 2018 for energy sector development in Nepal:
	  – Facilitate wider deployment of renewable energy including wind, solar, mini/micro hydel.
	  – Use of off-grid, community-based and low carbon electricity supply will be high priority.
	• Renewal Energy for Rural Livelihood (RERL), UNDP, 2014.
	• Nepal Energy Sector Development Policy Credit (2018–2020), World Bank.
	• Nepal Power System Reform and Sustainable Hydropower Development, World Bank.
	• Nepal Grid Solar and Energy Efficiency Project, World Bank.
	• Extended Biogas Project, World Bank.

Recommendations for attaining IGG goal in sustainable energy	• Support in the establishment or strengthening of safeguard section in government agencies in energy sector (Alternate Energy Promotion Center, Project Management Directorate, Nepal Electricity Authority). • Institutional strengthening and capacity building of federal, provincial, and local government on environment friendly development, shifting toward IGG, database preparation, and monitoring and enforcement. • Review the action plan suggested by ADB's Nepal Energy Sector Assessment, Strategy and Roadmap 2017 and strengthen environmental safeguards recommendations. • Support in climate change considerations through shifting energy modes with lower carbon emissions and through mainstreaming climate change in energy development and operation. • Rapid formation of GLOF due to climate change is a huge threat for hydropower systems. Collaborate with ICIMOD and formulate plan to minimize risk of GLOF on infrastructure. • Encourage renewable and alternate low-carbon energy sources, such as hydro, solar, and wind energy. Promote off-grid community-based micro hydropower and solar energy systems. • Develop national, environmental, and natural resource database and operationalize national environmental management information system for informed decisions. • Conduct SEA of energy development plan, identify cumulative impacts, recommend potential location of dam, and identify rivers that should be declared "dam free" and "protected area for fish." • Prepare transmission line master plan and use existing transmission line corridors with multiple stringing and as common right of way instead of constructing parallel lines that will cause cutting of forest trees. • Coordinate with neighboring countries to manage transboundary type of impacts, such as movement of fishes and other reptiles along interconnected river basins. • Provide wildlife crossings across canals passing through areas with wildlife movements. • Prepare knowledge products from past experience and replicate good lessons learned from country and regional experience.
ADB's comparative advantage	• ADB's in-house expertise and region-wide experience. • Established competence in hydropower and solar energy and close working relationships with executing agencies place ADB in a position to contribute meaningfully. • Proper operational policy through Nepal Energy Sector Assessment, Strategy and Roadmap 2017. • Knowledge on best practices. • Good record of attracting cofinancing. • Ability to move faster than competitors. • Capacity to attract climate finance.

Source: CIDENAR Study Team, 2019

Note: * This is not an exhaustive list.

Table VII-1-C: Sustainable Urban Services

Cities are the center of economic activity. However, the urban centers of Nepal are unplanned and organically grown with all sorts of environmental problems, such as air pollution, water pollution, unmanaged solid waste, shantytowns, and squatter settlements in unhygienic environment.

Broad outline of the sustainable urban services	• Support preparing sustainable and earthquake resistant urban development master plan for cities. • Support improving air, water, and noise quality in cities. • Support reviving highly polluted and ecologically dead rivers flowing through cities. • Support improving solid waste management in cities. • Support improving sanitation in urban settlements via climate-resilient wastewater treatment systems. • Support broader perspective on urban transportation, such as integration of land use and transportation, promotion of sustainable urban public transport, and development of transport management standards. • Promote adequate, reliable, efficient, and sustainable green energy in urban areas. • Help build urban environmental management awareness and capacity by mainstreaming environmental and climate change issues into decision-making.
Issues of concern while assessing IGG for sustainable urban development	• Federal governance structure has given authority to implement development projects to local bodies that do not have efficient and capable safeguard section, staff, and resources. This has tremendously increased the risk of overlooking environmental protection while implementing projects for urban development. • Polluting industries such as brick kilns, vehicular emission, and construction of roads, sewerage system and buildings are the key reasons of air quality deterioration in the urban areas. • Direct discharge of urban sewers in water bodies in cities is a major problem in polluting rivers in urban areas. • Lack of enforcement to control polluting behavior of urban residents. • Sustainability of urbanization in Nepal is threatened by a lack of effective planning and large and growing infrastructure deficits. • Urbanization of groundwater recharge areas has critically depleted groundwater table causing drought, dust, and land subsidence in urban areas. • Decreasing green cover and open areas in urban centers are choking the cities. • Unplanned urban development has led to rapid and uncontrolled sprawl; irregular, substandard, and inaccessible housing development; and loss of open space and decreased livability (Managing Nepal's Urban Transition, World Bank). • Urban centers are highly vulnerable to the impacts of climate change and disasters in the absence of climate resilient planning and adaptation.
Relevant action by ADB, Development Partners and Government*	• Melamchi Water Supply Project, ADB • Integrated Urban Development Project, ADB • Secondary Towns Integrated Urban Environmental Improvement Project • Kathmandu Valley Water Sector Improvement Project, ADB • Kathmandu Valley Wastewater Management Project, ADB • Regional Urban Development Project, ADB • Second and Third Small Towns Water Supply and Sanitation Sector Project, ADB • Bagmati River Basin Improvement Project, ADB • Building Resilience to Climate Related Hazards, World Bank • Urban Governance and Development Program, Emerging Town Projects, World Bank • Basic construction standards for settlement development, urban planning and building construction 2016, Nepal. • Nepal National Urban Development Strategy 2017.

Recommendations for attaining IGG goals in sustainable urban development	• Support in updating urban policy, and establish or strengthen safeguard section in government agencies (Ministry of Urban Development, Department of Urban Development and Building Construction), and provincial and local government (municipalities and rural municipalities). • Follow the action plan suggested by ADB's Urban Operational Plan 2012–2020. • Support urban areas use clean energy with lower carbon emissions. • Encourage vehicles to use renewable low-carbon energy sources, such as electric and solar energy. • Encourage infrastructure to promote non-motorized mode of transportation. • Support urban areas in using climate friendly technologies while managing solid waste and wastewater treatment. • Ban non-biodegradable waste, such as plastic products, and introduce 3R principle for waste management. • Improve quality of construction approach in urban areas by containing air, water, noise, and visual pollution. • Promote open areas and green cover through plantation. • Prepare knowledge products from past experience and replicate good lessons learned from country and regional experience.
ADB's comparative advantage	• ADB's in-house expertise and region-wide experience. • ADB's Urban Operational Plan 2012-2020. • ADB's Unleashing Economic Growth: Region-based Urban Development Strategy for Nepal, 2010, and Green Cities 2012. • ADB's vision for livable cities for safe and sustainable urban centers. • Knowledge on best practices. • Good record of attracting cofinancing. • Ability to move faster than competitors. • Capacity to attract climate finance.

Source: CIDENAR Study Team, 2019

Note: * This is not an exhaustive list.

B. Investing in Natural Capital

Ecosystems and biodiversity are on the decline in Asia and the Pacific. ADB and World Wildlife Fund (WWF) reported a 67% decline in the health of ecosystems in the region over the last 40 years, which was twice the global average.[96] South Asia's rich ecosystem is under immense threat from habitat loss, climate change, over exploitation, and pollution.[97]

Natural capital has been a key contributor to the country's economic growth. However, the key natural capital stocks are in a state of decline, as evidenced by the degradation of arable land; considerable losses in forests and wetlands; and endangered and/or extinct species of terrestrial, aquatic, and avian fauna and flora. Without the necessary economic signals, the exploitation of natural capital over the short term is often more financially attractive than nurturing it over the long term, ultimately compromising prospects for sustainable development. Investing in

natural capital can have high returns, and is typically more cost-effective than restoring degraded ecosystem.[98] ADB's Safeguard Policy Statement (2009) aims to ensure that ADB-supported projects use natural resources in a sustainable manner and are achieved with a minimum or no net loss of biodiversity.

The management of natural capital includes the following three thematic areas:

Theme 1: Sustainable and resilient forest and natural resource management

Theme 2: Agriculture and food security

Theme 3: Integrated water resource management

---

[96] ADB and WWF. 2012. *Ecological Footprint and Investment in Natural Capital in Asia and the Pacific.* Manila.
[97] N. Ahmed. 2013. *Asian Development Blog: Why Invest in Natural Capital.* 22 April. Manila.
[98] See footnote 86.

Table VII-2-A: Forest and Natural Resource Management

Sustainable and resilient management of forest and other natural resources can provide a basis for sustaining local livelihoods, clean water supplies, and protection of biological diversity. The approach should be to protect and manage the full range of ecosystem services that can increase climate resilience by reducing the intensity of floods and droughts and enhancing the ecosystem services provided by forests and other natural ecosystems.

Broad outline of the sustainable forest, natural resources, and land use component of IGG	• Forest policy, act, and regulation. Forest policy updated in 2019. Update act and regulation for forest and natural resource management considering the new federal governance structure. • The three levels of governance under the new federal government system face challenges in sustainable development due to lack of a functional and capacitated safeguard unit in their respective institutions. • Protect forests to sustain biodiversity, improve carbon sequestration, and link economic benefits and livelihood support through participatory mechanisms. • Indigenous and local forest and pasture management practices have evolved from cultural norms, traditional values, contextual demand, collective effort, community-based institutions, and a good understanding of local ecosystems. • Lack of meaningful and visual compensatory plantation by infrastructure development projects. • Improve forest and watershed management to protect livelihood, water, and biodiversity. • Nepal lacks sufficient negotiation skills in marketing of natural resource protection for economic benefit in international market through payment for ecosystem services (PES). • Increase climate resilience to reduce the intensity of floods and droughts through ecosystem-based approaches. • Infrastructure routing through protected wildlife habitats, conservation area, and movement corridors. • Conserve natural capital through strict implementation of land use policy, act, and regulation. • Conserve highly vulnerable ecological zones of the country, such as the Chure Hills. • Promote community-based natural resource and biodiversity protection. • Act on Forestry Sector Policy of Nepal 2000, and biodiversity conservation strategy. • Promote energy sector reform and capacity building in sustainable forest management.
Issues of concern while assessing IGG for sustainable natural resources and land use	• The federal governance structure has given authority to implement development projects to local bodies that do not have a safeguard section, staff, and resources. This has tremendously increased the risk of overlooking environmental protection while implementing projects. The risk of deforestation, encroachment, and degradation of land use has increased. • The 2015 Constitution has placed national forests under the provincial governments but also listed national forests as the common right of federal, provincial, and local governments. The Local Government Operation Act 2017 provided rural municipalities the right to protect, use, manage, monitor, regulate, formulate, and implement laws. These overlapping roles cause confusion. • Policies, acts, and regulations need to be updated in the context of new federal governance structure with local bodies and provinces responsible to implement development infrastructure and natural resource management. • A new forestry sector master plan is needed to replace the plan of 1998. • Recognize and promote community participatory mechanisms in management of local natural resources such as forest and water. • General tendency to align roads and transmission lines along forests avoiding private land has caused widespread tree cutting and forest stratification, watershed degradation, erosion and landslides, and loss of habitat. • Private crusher plant operators do not care about environmental degradation and practice over extraction of riverbed aggregates in vulnerable ecological areas, such as Chure and Mahabharat hills. Such activities are devastating the riparian ecosystem causing riverbed aggradation and degradation, floods, landslides and bank cutting, and loss of forest and wildlife habitats. • Encroachment in forest area by various interest groups (clubs, religious groups, security, squatters) supported by political parties has been one of the reasons for land use change and decline in forest area. • Illegal trade of forest products, herbs, and medicinal and aromatic plants. • Projects do not comply to compensatory plantation, despite a working procedure issued by the Ministry of Forest and Environment to plant 10 trees for each tree cleared from the forest. The directive has also given an alternative to deposit the amount required for planting trees and guarding them for 5 years in the account of district forest office. Cash option is followed by most of the projects to avoid complications associated with compresatory plantation.

Relevant action by ADB, Development Partners and Government*	• Building climate resilience of watersheds in mountain eco-regions is supporting the protection of watershed and conservation of water sources, ADB. • Leasehold Forestry and Livestock Program, LFLP (1992–2012) supported by International Fund for Agricultural Development (IFAD). • Forestry Sector Strategy (2016–2025), Nepal. • Nepal National REDD+ Strategy (reduction of emission from deforestation and forest degradation). • Multi-stakeholder Forestry Program, Department for International Development of the United Kingdom (DFID 2016). • Livelihoods and Forestry Program, DFID (2012). • Hariyo Ban Project, USAID. • Nepal has a full set of required policies, acts, regulations, and strategies to manage forests, biodiversity, and natural resources. Capacity to strictly implement them and weaknesses in overcoming political pressure are some of the issues that can lead to degradation of forest and biodiversity.
Recommendations for attaining IGG goal in sustainable forest and land use	• Update policies, acts, regulations, and strategies to make them relevant under the newly formed federal structure of governance. Provincial and local bodies should formulate harmonized local policies that are participatory, inclusive, environment friendly, and resilient to the risks of climate change to conserve natural resources (forest, land, and biodiversity). Increase investment in sustainable natural resource, including Chure conservation, flood protection, regeneration of urban river ecosystem, watershed management, and protection of land and forests. • Institutional strengthening and capacity building of safeguard sections in federal, provincial, and local governments on environmental protection through planning, monitoring, and enforcement. • Protect forest for carbon sequestration and link with financial benefits to the community, such as watershed conservation and promotion of REDD+ program; support in economic valuation of ecosystem-based services and help in their marketing. Leverage the national and regional natural resource conservation initiatives through collaboration, such as in upscaling investment in climate change to protect Himalayan glaciers and prevent GLOF, and in protecting biodiversity. • Take advantage of Terai Arc Landscape Programme (WWF) and Hariyo Ban project (USAID, WWF). • Conduct strategic environmental assessment of sector plans and policies, including forestry sector master plan, and implement all future programs under the scope of the master plan. • Develop national environmental and natural resource database repository and operationalize national environmental management information system to support informed decision-making. • Study the risks of climate change on fauna and flora. • Coordinate with neighboring countries in managing transboundary impacts, such as movement of fish and reptiles along interconnected river basins, and the impact of damming for hydropower and irrigation. • Maintain biological corridors and inclusion of wildlife viaducts in infrastructures, such as canals, roads, and reservoirs passing through or located in forest areas with wildlife habitat. • Invest in conservation of Chure hills by implementing the Chure Conservation Master Plan. • Mainstream community livelihood in natural resource management component of projects, such as eco-tourism, community forestry, eco-savior clubs, and management of human—wildlife conflict. • Support the strengthening of country safeguard system involving federal, provincial, and local governments. • Prepare knowledge products from past experience and replicate good lessons learned from country and regional experience.
ADB's comparative advantage	• ADB's in-house expertise and region-wide experience. • Established competence in hydropower and solar energy and close working relationships with executing agencies place ADB in a position to contribute meaningfully. • Fish screening framework recommended by ADB's Study on Impact of Dams on Fish in the Rivers of Nepal, 2019. • Knowledge on international best practices. • Good record of attracting cofinancing. • Ability to move faster than competitors. • Capacity to attract climate finance.

Source: CIDENAR Study Team, 2019

Note: * This is not an exhaustive list.

Table VII-2-B: Agriculture and Food Security

Broad outline of sustainable agriculture and food security	• Agriculture Development Strategy 2015 of government that address agriculture development and food security • Promote diversified and climate-resilient crop production and development of value chains. • Cascade climate change impact modeling and analysis of associated risks across target regions, sectors, and communities for climate resilient farming. • Community-based climate impact assessment of target watersheds, vulnerable watershed-dependent populations, and agriculture infrastructure. • Climate-adaptive agribusiness and livelihood technology packages. • Enhance capacity of vulnerable rural communities and local producer organizations to operationalize the climate-adaptive technology package.
Issues of concern while assessing IGG for sustainable agriculture and food security	• The federal governance structure has given authority to implement agriculture development to local bodies that do not have safeguard sections, staff, and resources. This has tremendously increased the risk of weak management and degradation of natural resources. • Degradation of watershed and drying up of water sources could impact productivity and add pressure on food security. • Regulations and standards (enact controls on excessive use of agrochemicals in production). • Establish standards for water quality and land management. • Improve enforcement of environmental regulations in agriculture. • Support measures to decouple farm supports from production levels and prices, increase assistance to environmental practices, and extend environmental cross-compliance measures. • Research and development in green growth by agriculture sector.

Relevant action by ADB, Development Partners and Government*	• The recent ADB projects under this theme are irrigation, drainage, flood protection, water-based natural resource management, and agriculture and rural sector development.
	• Rural Connectivity Improvement Project (2018–2020), ADB.
	• Decentralized Rural Infrastructure and Livelihood Project, ADB.
	• Rural Access Program (RAP-III), Department for International Development (DFID).
	• Commercial Agriculture Development Project (CADP), which used a grant funding approach for Commercial Agriculture Alliance (CAA) to fund private sector development.
	• Project to strengthen the national rural transport program, World Bank.
	• Value Chain, Himali Project (2011-2018), ADB.
	• Support for Value Chain Development under the Nepal Agriculture Development Strategy (2015).
	• There are a number of development partner-supported programs and projects which focus on value chain and agribusiness in Nepal, and these are:
	  – IFAD High Value Agriculture Project (HVAP);
	  – SNV working with IFAD on HVAP;
	  – IFAD Western Upland Poverty Evaluation Project (WUPAP), which is involved in value chain support in the districts of western Nepal;
	  – EU/FAO funded Food Facility Project with an emphasis on food security; and
	  – Nepal Food Security Project, World Bank.

Recommendations for attaining IGG goal in sustainable agriculture and food security	• Support agriculture development investments under the government's agriculture development strategy. • Introduce diversified and climate resistant crop varieties. • Develop a value chain supported by improved market access. • Manage water resource with watershed conservation, source protection, water conservation, and equitable distribution. • Support in developing green supply chain. • Support medium farmers-managed irrigation system rehabilitation to provide direct economic benefits to small farmers. • Invest in large irrigation projects for national food security and economic development.
ADB's comparative advantage	• ADB's in-house expertise and region-wide experience. • Close working relationships with executing agencies place ADB in a position to contribute meaningfully. • Knowledge on best practices. • Good record of attracting cofinancing. • Ability to move faster than competitors. • Capacity to attract climate finance.

Source: CIDENAR Study Team, 2019

Note: * This is not an exhaustive list.

Table VII-2-C: Integrated Water Resources Management

Water is a critical issue to sustainable economic development. The water sector needs an integrated management approach since water security, energy security, and food security are inextricably linked and actions in one area, more often than not, have impacts on other areas. This is the concept of the water-energy-food nexus. Integrated water resources management (IWRM) is a process to improve the planning, conservation, development, and management of water, forest, land, and aquatic resources in a river basin context. The water, energy, and food nexus should also be taken into account while planning integrated water resource management.

Broad outline of the integrated water resource management	<ul><li>Nepal has abundant water resource with 6,000 rivers and capacity to generate 43,000-MW hydropower.</li><li>Availability of 225 billion cubic meters of water, but only 15 billion cubic meters are used.</li><li>72% of the population has access to clean water.</li><li>The estimated total direct annual economic cost of water-induced disasters is US$270 million per year on average, equivalent to 1.5% of Nepal's current gross domestic product (GDP).</li><li>Economic loss due to the impact of climate change on water resources and energy production could be 0.1% of GDP per year.</li><li>Strengthening water resource management is essentially a public sector responsibility.</li><li>The government has formulated several policies and regulations to manage water resources in Nepal. The policies aim to regulate water use, increase access to water for drinking and irrigation, and maximize the benefits of abundance of water resources for hydropower generation.</li><li>Nepal's judicial system is relevant for water governance as it deals with managing the conflict and disputes arising from water management.</li><li>Water Resources Strategy Nepal 2002 is a cross-cutting document that sets out a comprehensive approach to water planning.</li><li>Water Resources Act 1996 aims to make arrangements for the rational utilization, conservation, management, and development of water resources.</li><li>National Water Plan 2005 recognizes the objectives of the national water strategy (NWS) and lays down short-, medium-, and long-term action plans for the water resources development</li><li>Hydropower Development Policy 2001 lacks reference to the potential impacts of climate change on hydrological flows or competing water demands.</li><li>At the national level, there are conflicting roles and responsibilities among the institutions working on water sector. Despite the presence of the Water and Energy Commission (WEC), institutional confusion exists in dealing with integrated national water issues.</li><li>Water institutions are of four categories: (i) policy/planning and coordinating bodies, (ii) sector policy, planning and programming organizations, (iii) regulatory bodies, and (iv) service providers with autonomous nature, including local bodies.</li><li>Overlapping institutional responsibilities and lack of clarity of roles within the central water resource management ministry, departments and offices often lead to ineffective translation of policies (D.N. Dhungel. 2016. *Policies and Institutions on Water Resources – Nepal*).</li><li>Increasing population, rapid urbanization, and competing demand for water for domestic use, agriculture, and energy have left water stocks in a critical state.</li><li>Conservation of highly vulnerable ecological zones and watersheds is vital for protecting water sources.</li></ul>

	• The Water Resources Strategy Nepal and the National Water Plan called for integrated water resources strategy by reconciling all water policies, but this is yet to be done. The government instead started preparing sector policies and legislation in isolation. The country still lacks an integrated water resources policy and act. Federalization of governance system has further complicated water basin and water resource management.
	• The formation of National Water Resources Development Council in 1993 was an extremely important milestone in water resources development. The council, dominated by political actors, was expected to be a "mini-parliament," where water issues would be debated to ultimately arrive at how this resource should be used in different sectors in a coordinated manner, and also with the neighboring countries. However, the council has remained inactive since then.
	• Weak cooperation, consultation, and working modalities have left the regional level of integrated water basin planning in a limbo.
	• The ministries of energy and irrigation were merged in 2017 as the Ministry of Energy, Water Resources and Irrigation, paving the way to integrated planning. However, the policies, plans, and strategies are still fragmented, and they do not consider integrated water resource management at basin level and do not address water, forest, land, and agriculture as inter-related components.
Issues of concern while assessing integrated water resources management	• The concept of IWRM is not fully internalized in the existing water planning and programming system.
	• Political decisions are limited to water use and distribution, and do not take into account resources management and conservation.
	• Groundwater pollution from urban and industrial waste is rapidly becoming a serious problem, and remedial measures are difficult and costly.
	• Joint use of surface and groundwater for year-round irrigation is yet to be fully explored.
	• Climate change impact has become critical in diminishing water security and increasing water- induced disasters. Global warming causing melting of ice in the Himalayas and retreating glaciers indicates huge threat to billions of downstream population dependent on the water stored in the ice caps. Nepal is not yet equipped and capacitated to study, analyze, and predict the impacts of climate change. Weak preparation to combat water insecurity as a result of climate change has rendered the communities highly vulnerable to diminishing water access. Villages are reported to be abandoning their ancestral land due to drying up of water sources.
	• Federal governance structure has given authority to implement development projects to local bodies that do not have safeguard sections, staff, and resources. This has tremendously increased the risk of overlooking environmental protection while implementing projects. The risk of polluting water bodies, unsustainable groundwater extraction, and encroachment could increase without government monitoring and enforcement.
	• Lack of knowledge and capacity to rightly address the water-energy-food nexus, which may drive the country toward food deficiency and increased poverty.
Relevant action by ADB, Development Partners and Government*	• Building climate resilience of watersheds in mountain eco-regions is supporting the protection of watershed and conservation of water sources, ADB.
	• The Bagmati River Basin Improvement Project aims to establish a river basin organization to integrate river basin management of the Bagmati river, ADB.
	• The Water Resources Project Preparatory Facility supported Nepal in formulating integrated water resources management policy, act, and regulation, ADB.

Recommendations for attaining IGG goal in integrated water resource management	• Formulate and urgently adopt the IWRM policy, act, and regulation. Policies, laws, and institutions need reform to meet today's challenges in the sector. • Establish coordination in basin-wide planning and implementation of water use among the provinces under a given river basin. Then, establish a river basin organization (RBO) with representation from federal, provincial, and local governments, and other stakeholders and beneficiaries to generate a common vision with collective and coordinated efforts at all levels. • Institutional strengthening and capacity building of water resources section in federal, provincial, and local governments to improve integrated water resources management. • Introduce IWRM and undertake comprehensive water resource assessments in river basins as a basis for water investment projects. These assessments allow better understanding of the links between water and land use, the environment, and sustainable development. • Use GIS and remote sensing technologies along with modeling to design water management project. • Encourage nature-based solutions, such as wetland promotion, "room for the river," sponge cities, risk reduction, flood forecasting and early warning, land use planning as a means to optimize investment. • Manage the risks of floods to people, land and infrastructure through informed decision-making for investment and financing, and formulate measures and instruments to reduce disaster risk in an efficient and sustainable manner. • Promote adaptability by identifying what could be modified or adapted in response to future (or uncertain) changes or in response to new knowledge, as a means of optimizing investments. • The government may change its role from service provider to regulator for better delivery of water services. • Promote partnerships between governments, private agencies, NGOs, and communities. Facilitate NGOs to play a key role in catalyzing critical water sector reforms and the necessary public awareness. • Strengthen WEC as the national apex body to coordinate IWRM reform and formulate a national water action agenda. • Maximize economic benefits and social welfare in an equitable manner without compromising the sustainability of vital environmental systems. • Address quantity and quality concerns for surface and groundwater, and plan for their conjunctive use. • Promote the formulation of national water policies and river basin management to improve water allocation. • Since water is a socially vital economic good, systems need to be introduced to value water in all its uses as a basis for allocation among competing users. This is particularly crucial during water stress and severe scarcity. • Rehabilitate watersheds with participatory involvement of local communities and NGOs. Wetlands have important functions in the river basin, including flood alleviation, groundwater recharge, water quality improvement, ecosystem maintenance, and biodiversity conservation. Hence, promote wetland conservation and improvement in a river basin context. • Promote sustainable groundwater management as an integral element of water resources management. • Prepare knowledge products from past experience and replicate good lessons learned from country and regional experience.
ADB's comparative advantage	• ADB's in-house expertise and region-wide experience in integrated water resource development. • Established competence in water resources sector and close working relationships with executing agencies place ADB in a position to contribute meaningfully. • Proper guiding policy through ADB's Water Operational Plan 2011–2020. • With ADB's ability, neutrality, and comparative advantage in providing assistance, it is better poised to assist governments in developing collaborative frameworks with riparian stakeholders. • Knowledge on international best practices. • Good record of attracting cofinancing. • Ability to move faster than competitors. • Capacity to attract climate finance.

Source: CIDENAR Study Team, 2019

Note: * This is not an exhaustive list.

C. Strengthening Environmental Governance and Management Capacity

Nepal has established policy, legal, and institutional frameworks to promote sustainable development, and is a party to most of the environment, biodiversity, and climate change conventions and multilateral agreements. However, despite its comparatively sound policy framework and institutional setup, actual reform and implementation has been weak due to limited institutional capacity, lack of technical expertise, insufficient funding, and fragmented responsibilities. Policymakers and decision-makers do not have sufficient database for informed decision-making. Many acts and regulations are obsolete and require updating due to evolving context. The plans and programs—although good on paper—their implementation, monitoring, and enforcement have been weak, which is further exacerbated by the fluid socio-political context in the country over the last 2 decades.

The environmental governance and management include the following thematic areas for transition toward IGG:

Theme 1: Policy and incentive framework
Theme 2: Compliance and enforcement
Theme 3: Strengthening of environmental safeguard capacity

Environmental governance could improve if institutions are established with required resources, and if their mandate for good governance is supported by legal provisions and capacity to implement them. Table VII-3 covers the three thematic areas and provides actionable recommendations.

Table VII 3. Strengthening Environmental Governance and Management Capacity

Broad outline of the environmental governance and management • Policy and incentive framework • Compliance and enforcement • Strengthening of environmental safeguard capacity	• Formulate legal policies, acts, and regulations to conserve environment and natural resources in harmony among the national, provincial, and local levels. • Many legal provisions and strategies related with environment, climate change and biodiversity are awaiting government approval. • Lack of functional, capable, and resourced government safeguard institutions at all levels. • Nepal lacks sufficient capacity to negotiate payment for ecosystem services in international market for carbon sequestration through forest conservation • Implement nature conservation management programs linked with community livelihood. • Increase climate resilience to reduce the intensity of floods and droughts through ecosystem-based approaches. • Conserve highly vulnerable, special ecological areas such as the Chure hills.

Issues of concern while assessing IGG for environmental governance and management • Policy and incentive framework • Compliance and enforcement • Strengthening of environmental safeguard capacity	• The federal governance structure has given authority to implement development projects to provincial and local bodies those do not have proper safeguard institutional arrangement, staff, capacity and resources. Hence their role in environmental safeguard monitoring and enforcement has been absent or critically weak. This has tremendously increased the risk of environmental degradation and loss of biodiversity. • Many policies, acts, and regulations need to be updated and harmonized in the context of new federal government structure. • Environmental sector strategy and guidelines are either missing or obsolete (energy, irrigation, forest, aquatic biodiversity), and require updating in the context of the new governance system. Similarly, no safeguard units have been established in key infrastructure development agencies (ministries, departments), and this has caused weak monitoring and enforcement, and overlooking of key safeguards provisions while preparing national policies, projects, and programs. • Many legal provisions are waiting implementation such as REDD+ strategy and implementation plan, Nepal biodiversity strategy and action plan, forest investment program, and emission reduction program. Few strategies have been drafted, and are yet to be endorsed by the government. These include national pollution control strategy and action plan, and low carbon economic development strategy. These provisions should be urgently adopted and implemented to realize the goal to shift toward IGG. • Environmental challenges and climate change risks are transboundary requiring legal provisions and cooperation at the regional level. • Lack of baseline database is the largest hindrance in preparing informed, environment friendly, and climate resilient plan, policy, and program. Information will be increasingly scattered and de-linked between national, provincial, and local governments if a collective information repository and sharing system is not developed. • Current legal provisions make environmental assessment of development projects mandatory, however monitoring and enforcement and action for corrective measures are missing. As a result, project developers escape without complying with environmental requirements. • Lack of safeguard orientation among government agencies, proper safeguard training program for government staff, budget, and competitive agencies in Nepal. • Lack of capacity of the government to tap regional knowledge sharing and financing programs.

Relevant action by ADB, Development Partners and Government*	• ADB support in drafting national pollution control strategy and action plan (awaiting cabinet approval).
	• Environmental safeguards compliance in project planning, preparation, and implementation strengthened through regular training by ADB's capacity development resource center.
	• Building climate resilience of watersheds in mountain eco-regions is supporting the protection of watershed and conservation of water sources, ADB
	• President Chure—Tarai Madhesh conservation and Management Master Plan, Nepal
	• Forestry Sector Strategy (2016–2025), Nepal.
	   – Forest productivity and sustainable supplies of products and services
	   – Biodiversity, watersheds, and ecosystem services improvement
	   – Organizational and institutional development in forestry sector
	   – Climate resilient capacity of society and forest ecosystem
	   – Livelihood and forestry sector contributions to national economic development
	• Nepal National REDD+ Strategy (draft).
	• Multi-stakeholder Forestry Program, DFID (2016).
	• Hariyo Ban Project, USAID.

Recommendations for attaining IGG goal in strengthening environmental governance and management	• Update policies, acts, regulations, and strategies to make them relevant under the newly formed federal structure of governance. Provincial and local bodies require support in formulating local- level policies that are environment friendly and resilient to climate change risks to conserve forest and biodiversity. The legal provisions should make public monitoring and enforcement mandatory with punitive actions, and integrate the provisions. • Establish fully resourced and functional safeguard institutions with full staffing and budget at all three levels of the government. Support them and build capacity on environmental governance, shifting toward IGG. • Adopt and implement REDD+ strategy, Nepal biodiversity strategy and action plan, forestry sector policy, Chure conservation master plan, emission reduction program, national pollution control strategy and action plan, and low carbon economic development strategy. • Build negotiation capacity of community in marketing of natural resource conservation to economically benefit from payment for ecosystem services. • Continue and build upon the successful results of nature conservation management, such as the highly successful participatory community forest management, participatory buffer zone management, and leasehold forestry. • Build on the efforts to conserve highly vulnerable ecological zones, such as Chure, and prevent river aggradation and flooding, drying of water sources, and desertification of land. • Initiate and improve regional consultation, cooperation, and strategic partnership in addressing transboundary environmental impacts. • Prepare national, environmental, and natural resource database and operationalize national environmental management information system for informed decision-making. • Support the strengthening of country safeguard system covering federal, provincial, and local governments.
ADB's comparative advantage	• ADB's in-house expertise and region-wide experience. • Close working relationships with executing agencies place ADB in a position to contribute meaningfully. • Knowledge on best practices. • Good record of attracting cofinancing. • Ability to move faster than competitors. • Capacity to attract climate finance.

Source: CIDENAR Study Team, 2019

Note: * This is not an exhaustive list.

D. Responding to the Climate Change Imperative

As climate change impacts increase, Nepal's vulnerability will continue to grow. About 80% of Nepal's population lives in the rural areas, hence improving the resilience of the villages and communities to the risks of climate change is crucial. Around 70% of Nepal's population depends on agriculture, which is affected by changes in climatic conditions, affecting lives and livelihoods of the farmers and causing food security risks. The increased rate of glacial melting and risks of GLOF, and decrease in snow reserve in the Himalayas not only threatens Nepal but also affects the billions living downstream in the South Asian rivers and delta basin. Such far-reaching consequences of climatic change can undermine development and reverse the hard-earned development gains. Addressing current and future risks requires a comprehensive preparedness program, including integration of preparedness in development programming, and a solid repository of knowledge and trained human resources.

The climate change response actions—both adaptation and mitigation—will cut across the other three components (sustainable infrastructure, investment in natural capital, and environmental governance), and needs to be fully integrated with each component.[99]

Theme 1: Capacity building and support to Nepal in climate change plan, policy, and programs

Theme 2: Ecosystem-based adaptation to climate change and other natural risks

---

[99] ADB. 2010. *Focused Action: Priorities for Addressing Climate Change in Asia and the Pacific.* Manila.

Table VII-4: Responding to the Climate Change Imperative

Broad outline of the climate change imperative • Capacity building and support to Nepal in climate change plan, policy, and programs • Ecosystem-based adaptation to climate change and other natural risks and reduction of community vulnerability through participatory approach • Scaling up provision of off-grid decentralized renewable energy	• Support integrated approach to address climate change mitigation and adaptation by mobilizing financing, generating knowledge, building partnership, and transferring climate-friendly technologies (IGG 2013, ADB). • Nepal has formulated the national climate change policy 2019, national adaptation plan of actions (NAPA 2010) and local adaptation plan of actions (LAPA 2011), climate change planning tool 2012 and budget code 2012, nationally determined contribution 2016; and established a focal institution to address climate change and manage risks. Nepal is a party to the United Nations Framework Convention on Climate Change (UNFCCC). • Update and formulate acts and regulations for reducing carbon and greenhouse gas emission that are uniformly applicable at the national, provincial, and local levels. • Climate change institutions are needed in all three levels of government. • Increasing vulnerability of the poor due to the impacts of climate change. • There are existing indigenous and local knowledge and practices in adapting to the risks of climate change (Indigenous and Local Knowledge and Practices for Climate Resilience in Nepal, ADB 2013. • National and local adaptation plan of action (NAPA and LAPA) has been prepared. • Weak stakeholder capacity in mainstreaming climate change risks in development. • Use of biomass (firewood and dung) in rural areas and weak off-grid energy solution. • Limited initiative to access climate change funds.
Issues of concern while assessing IGG for climate change imperative	• The federal governance structure has given authority to implement development projects to provincial and local bodies that do not have a institutional arrangement for safeguards, staff, capacity and resources. They lack sufficient knowledge on mitigation measures and adaptation to the risks of climate change. • Rising GHG and black carbon emission increases temperature in the Himalayan ecological region. • Establish fully resourced and functional climate change institution with staffing and budget at all three levels of government, major infrastructure and natural resource ministries, and local bodies. • Adopt the low carbon economic development strategy (in draft stage). • Existing policy and action plans (NAPA, LAPA) need updating and harmonization with the federal governance system. • Lack of complete and improved system of climatic data monitoring, recording, and dissemination facility.
Relevant action by ADB, Development Partners and Government*	• Mainstreaming Climate Change Risk Management in Development, ADB (2013–2018). • Building climate resilience of watersheds in mountain eco-regions, ADB (2013–2020). • Nepal Climate Change Support Program, UNDP and DFID, UK • Minimize climate change impact on agriculture, UNDP and the Food and Agriculture Organization of the United Nations (FAO), funded by the Government of Germany under International Climate Initiative. • Support in Scaling up Renewable Energy Program. • Ecosystem-based adaptation in mountain ecosystems in Nepal (2012–2015), UNDP through Department of Forest. • Nepal Climate Change Support Program, UNDP (2013–2015). • SASEC Power Sector Enhancement Project (off-grid component). • Energy Access and Efficiency Improvement Project, ADB. • Renewable Energy for Rural Livelihood (RERL) Green Environment Fund/UNDP (2011–2014). • Nepal Biogas Support Program (BSP), SNV, Netherlands • Nepal Biogas Program, World Bank (2015). • Nepal-village Micro hydro, World Bank (2015). • Government completing community vulnerability assessment to the risks of climate change; and preparing national Adaptation Plan

Recommendations for attaining IGG goal in climate change imperative	• Support strengthening of environmental governance and climate change risk assessment capacity at national, provincial, and local levels. Establish fully resourced and functional climate change unit with staffing and budget at all three levels of government. • Update policies, acts, regulations, and strategies on climate change to make them relevant under the newly formed federal governance. Provincial and local bodies require support in formulating local policies that are climate resilient and environment friendly. • Strengthen public sector capacity in mainstreaming climate change risks in the project cycle to climate proof infrastructures. Embed climate change risks from initial stage of project processing through risk screening and assessment of climate change impact, vulnerability, and adaptation. • Upscale indigenous knowledge of vulnerable communities on adaptation to the risks of climate change. Use recommendations provided by Indigenous and Local Knowledge and Practices for Climate Resilience in Nepal (ADB TA-7984). • Accelerate off-grid renewable energy solutions (such as solar energy) and use of small and mini- hydropower in rural areas. • Promote activities that capitalize on ecosystem-inherent resilience to natural risks to protect and enhance livelihoods. Restore damaged ecosystems to reduce disaster risks. • Support the Department of Hydrology and Meteorology in preparing database on climate indicators. • Update and/or formulate climate change policy (NAPA and LAPA) that is applicable in the context of federal governance system. Implement recommendations of NAPA and LAPA. • Initiate and improve regional consultation, cooperation, and strategic partnership, and complement them with legal provisions, such as a memorandum of understanding. • Support Nepal in international climate change negotiations related to mitigation, adaptation, financing, and technology. • Discourage the use of fossil fuel and expand use of clean renewable energy. • Control emission of black carbon by substituting the use of biomass with improved cooking stoves, applying particle filters in diesel engines, promoting the use of biogas, and restricting open-field burning of agricultural waste. • Promote sustainable transport, water management, and urban development. • Promote watershed conservation and forest and natural resource management to maximize carbon sequestration, and bring them to international market for payment for carbon sink. • Conduct a study on the risks of climate change on natural resources and biodiversity of different ecological regions and implement mitigation plan. • Access financial instruments for climate change adaptation and resilience building, such as climate investment fund, global environment facility, green climate fund, and ADB's climate change fund, among others. • Develop monitoring, verification, and reporting systems to track result of policies and public investments. • Prepare knowledge products from past experience and replicate good lessons from country and regional experience.
ADB's comparative advantage	• ADB's in-house expertise and long and substantial experience in on- or off-grid energy solutions and renewable energy. • Established competence in hydropower and solar energy and close working relationships with executing agencies place ADB in a position to contribute meaningfully. • Proper operational policy through Nepal Energy Sector Assessment, Strategy and Roadmap 2017. • Strengthen designated agency for alternative energy promotion. • Knowledge on best practices, strong climate change policies, and ADB's Climate Change Operational Framework (2017–2030). • Experience in ecosystem conservation and restoration finance. • Capacity and experience to attract climate finance (climate investment fund, global environment facility, Green Climate Fund), availability of ADB climate fund, and opportunity to collaborate with other development partners in climate change financing.

Source: CIDENAR Study Team, 2019

Note: * This is not an exhaustive list.

VIII. ROLE OF DEVELOPMENT PARTNERS IN SAFEGUARDS

A. ADB's Assistance in Environment, Climate Change, and Disaster Risk Management in Nepal

ADB's assistance mainstreams environmental safeguards and adaptation to the risks of climate change in its investments. According to its CPS 2013–2017, ADB seeks to build institutional capacities ensuring implementation of environmentally safe and climate-friendly infrastructure by using risk-screening tools while processing the projects, which also aligns with the goals of the new CPS 2020-2024. ADB's assistance in environment and climate change focuses on the projects belonging to multiple sectors, particularly the transport, energy, urban, and water sectors; while disaster risk management primarily focuses on education (school buildings), access to post-disaster relief, and water resources (flood risk management infrastructure). Urban environment improvement projects focus on improving urban environment and sanitation. These projects include the Melamchi Water Supply Project (2000-2019) and Additional Financing (2014-2019), the Bagmati River Basin Improvement Project (2013–2020), the L2650 Secondary Towns Integrated Urban Environment Improvement Project (2011–2019), the Integrated Urban Development Project (2012–2019), the Kathmandu Valley Water Supply Improvement Project and Additional Financing (2015-2020), the Kathmandu Valley Wastewater Management Project (2013-2021), and the Urban Water Supply and Sanitation (Sector) Project (2018-2024). In the transport sector, the SASEC Road Connectivity Project (2014–2019), the SASEC Road Improvement Project (2016-2022) and the SASEC Highway Improvement Project (2018-2024) address biodiversity and greenery management. Energy projects such as the SASEC Power System Expansion Project (2015–2022) and the Tanahu Hydropower Project (2014–2021) have strictly complied with the required environmental management plan.

ADB has supported Nepal in climate change adaptation and resilience through various projects, such as the ongoing Building Climate Resilience Watersheds in Mountain Eco-Regions (2013-2020) which has helped build communities' resilience through protection of watershed and water sources. ADB has supported Nepal's government agencies in developing their capacity, in mainstreaming climate change risks, and in managing development operation through a technical assistance support (Mainstreaming Climate Change Risk Management in Development and Strengthening Capacity for Managing Climate Change and Environment).

ADB supported Nepal in building disaster risk resilience through various projects including the Earthquake Emergency Assistance Project (2015–2019) which helped in rebuilding and upgrading of schools, rehabilitation and reconstruction of roads and bridges, construction and rebuilding of district-level government facilities, and strengthening of disaster preparedness and management capacities; and the Disaster Resilience of School Project (2018–2023) which provides assistance in the rehabilitation of school buildings damaged by earthquake.[100]

Among the lessons learned in project implementation in Nepal for achieving sustainable development goals include the urgent improvement in policy and regulation, institutional mechanism at all three federal layers of government, and stringent enforcement for environmental protection. Also required are multi-stakeholder approach in increasing disaster and climate risk awareness, communicating DRM issues more effectively due to a challenging political and institutional environment, prioritizing capacity development to address weak institutional capacity in DRM, ensuring effective coordination mechanism especially with DRM champions and technical experts, and urgent need to invest in conservation of natural capital.

---

[100] ADB. 2015. *Report and Recommendation of the President to the Board of Directors: Proposed Loan and Technical Assistance Grant to Nepal for the Earthquake Emergency Assistance Project.* Manila.

B. Development Partners' Engagement in Environment, Climate Change, and Disaster Resilience Support in Nepal

The development partners of Nepal are supporting environment protection, climate change adaptation, and disaster risk management. The support is focused on improving policies, strengthening institutional mechanisms, reducing knowledge/technology gaps, imparting skills, and mainstreaming climate and disaster resilience in infrastructure projects.

The DFID, EU, Food and Agriculture Organization of the United Nations, IFAD, GIZ, JICA, SDC, UNDP, USAID, and World Bank, among others, are the major development partners supporting the Government of Nepal in environment, climate change, and disaster risk reduction activities in addition to other sectors. Most of them have mainstreamed environment and climate change in their programs and projects. Some of them are supporting in dedicated programs and projects related to environment protection, climate change mitigation, and disaster risk reduction.

The World Bank has included climate change as a cross-cutting theme in its Country Partnership Framework for Nepal in FY2019–2023. The Framework states that the Bank aims to meet the international development assistance policy commitment on climate change co-benefit, especially in operations that address energy, agriculture and livestock, forestry, trade and competitiveness, urban development, strategic and rural roads, and disaster risk management. It also incorporates, where appropriate, a contingent emergency response component. Linked to this effort to increase climate change co-benefit in projects, the World Bank supports Nepal in meeting its Nationally Determined Contributions commitments.

JICA is providing assistance to construct roads, hydropower, water facilities and other infrastructure; develop the private sector; establish legal, national, and social frameworks; and strengthen administrative capacity of government institutions. It also supports poverty reduction in rural areas through agriculture, education, and health services. JICA has ongoing projects in road and air transport, power generation, transmission and distribution capacity improvement, urban environment improvement, agriculture and rural development, and education and community health improvement. Many of the projects implemented by JICA are directly related to environmental protection, climate change adaptation, and disaster risk management.

The UNDP in Nepal focuses on energy, environment, climate change adaptation, and disaster risk management. UNDP helps mitigate and reduce the impact of climate change vulnerability and provides the rural poor with clean renewable energy and environment friendly livelihoods. A key part of UNDP's support across these areas is promoting pro-poor environmental management, risk reduction, and climate change adaptation at the national and local levels. DFID has supported in policy and climate resilient infrastructure through Nepal Climate Change Support Programme.

Natural resource conservation and utilization is one of Food and Agriculture Organization of the United Nations priority areas under which it contributes to enhancing the national capacity to promote improved sustainable management and development of natural resources, including land management, forestry and watershed management, climate resilient agriculture, and climate change mitigation and adaptation. USAID, Deutsche Gesellschaft für Internationale Zusammenarbeit, EU, SDC, and other development partners provide support in the areas of good governance, environment protection, climate change adaptation, and reduction of disaster risks.

IX. KEY ISSUES AND CHALLENGES

Nepal has made strides in inclusive green growth through supportive policy framework to meet the SDGs and sector policies in hydropower, agriculture, and infrastructure development. These key areas of intervention connect various policies, strategies, and plans related to sustainable development. Nepal's state of natural resources management and natural and cultural diversity and cooperation with neighboring countries offer unique opportunity for IGG. Nevertheless, Nepal faces score of environmental challenges to achieving sustainable development adopting the green growth strategy. Some of these challenges are discussed in the following subsections.

a. The Vicious Cycle of Poverty

Poverty is a major cause of environmental degradation. The poor families generally live in secluded, unsafe, and in a highly unsanitary and degraded environment—be it in rural or urban areas. They have to meet short-term needs by utilizing freely available natural resources. While people living in poverty are not the only creators of environmental damage, they become the principal victim of the consequences and are often caught in a downward spiral of poverty. The poor are forced to deplete resources to survive, and this causes degradation of the environment which further impoverishes them. When this self-reinforcing downward spiral becomes extreme, people are forced to move to marginal and ecologically fragile lands or to slums in cities with poor sanitation. Hence, poverty is a major cause of environmental degradation; and rapid economic growth and poverty alleviation are important in reversing the trend of environmental degradation.

b. Risk of Climate Change

Nepal faces the worst challenge from the global impacts of climate change. Erratic weather patterns, unpredictable and intense rainfall, reduced snowfall at high altitudes, recurrent droughts and floods, and a shift in the temperature regime have adversely affected agriculture and the livelihoods

of small farmers and poor people. The effects of climate change have been causing extreme hydrometeorological events triggering massive landslides and floods. Rapidly retreating glaciers in the Himalayas due to the effect of global warming has become one of the critical challenges in terms of glacial lake formation and increasing risks of GLOF. Climate scientists predict the continuation of more intense monsoons, and severe and frequent floods in the future.[101] Hence, the impacts of climate change is a major challenge faced by the country, which may jeopardize huge investments made in infrastructure development, decrease agricultural productivity, trigger disaster events and increase vulnerability of the poor—all leading toward deeper vicious cycle of poverty.

c. Risk of Natural Hazards

Nepal is at risk to disasters triggered by natural hazards including floods, landslides, droughts, and earthquakes. As climate change impacts increase, Nepal's vulnerability continues to grow. The loss of human lives and property due to natural hazards is one of the highest in Nepal. Poverty has dragged the poor into being seriously affected by natural disasters, such as earthquakes, floods, storms, and landslides. The poor usually live nearest to natural hazard prone areas, and this increases their scale of vulnerability. The effects of climate change such as sudden cloudbursts, floods, landslides, and droughts have further increased the risks of disaster. Deforestation, over exploitation of hill slope for unscientific farming and mining, riverbed aggregate extraction, improper use of chemical fertilizers and pesticides, settlements in vulnerable slopes, and city slums increase the poor communities' exposure and vulnerability leading to serious impacts in the event of a natural hazard. Some of the challenges in disaster risk management (DRM) include: (i) mainstreaming DRM in development planning, policies, and programs due to inadequate technical and functional capacities; (ii) silo approaches to DRM that do not recognize the interconnectedness of strategies and

---

[101] W. W. Immerzeel, L. P. Van Beek, and M. F. P. Bierkens. 2010. *Climate Change Will Affect the Asian Water Towers*. Science. 328 (5984). pp. 1382–1385.

actions in building resilience; (iii) financing challenges to invest adequately on DRM; (iv) poor DRM information and early warning systems; and (v) lack of appropriate risk assessments to support in planning.[102, 103, 104]

d. Rush syndrome in Energy Development

Nepal is the second-richest country in the world in water resources. In order to harness the natural resource for attaining prosperity, the government aims to develop 3,000 MW in 3 years; 5,000 MW in 5 years; and 15,000 MW of electricity in the next 10 years. The National Planning Commission unveiled the approach paper for the 15th periodic development plan with the long-term vision of graduating the country toward the status of middle-income country by 2043. The government aims to achieve the ambitious average economic growth rate of 10.1% during the plan period (Fiscal Year 2019/2020 to 2024/2025). In a rush to increase the pace of development to achieve the aim for prosperity, safeguards agenda may get sidelined causing a huge scale of project-specific, cumulative, and transboundary impacts. The government's decision to waive EIA for hydropower projects up to 50 MW irrespective of their ecological footprint and high rate of deforestation for infrastructure construction without a meaningful compensatory plantation are relevant examples of the impact of a rush syndrome.

e. New Federal Governments with Weak Institutional Capacity

The constitution has given the role and responsibility of infrastructure development to the newly formed provincial and local governments, which do not have a resourceful safeguard section and knowledgeable staff for environmental governance. This may cause huge environmental risks in the absence of institutional capacity to plan, implement, monitor, and enforce safeguards compliance in the development works. The unsuitable extraction of riverbed aggregates, mines and other natural resources, haphazard construction of non-engineered earthen roads on fragile hills, over extraction of groundwater in cities such as Kathmandu, and forest encroachments with sociopolitical protection are a few examples of such environmental risks.

f. Risk of Remittance-Steered Internal Migration

The rural population is currently enjoying a remittance-based economy that contributed more than 27.76% of the country's GDP in 2018. Most of the money flowing into the local levels is being used on unproductive investments such as buying land, vehicle, and property. Following the formation of local and provincial governments, the semi-rural townships have started to grow attracting internal migrants from the adjacent rural catchment areas supported by the remittance income. These townships are growing haphazardly in an unplanned manner. The migration from rural to urban areas has increased pressure on land, water, and vegetation in upcoming cities, whereas the productive agriculture fields in rural areas are being left uncultivated. Population pressure from migrants have worsened urban sanitation, water management, and transportation, and increased forest and public area encroachment. The situation will become worse and may spiral out of control if there is no urgent policy action for controlled urban growth.

g. Chure Degradation

Chure is a major source of livelihood of poor communities living there depending on the natural resources. Chure is also a source of water to the fertile Terai plain. However, the highly fragile geology is being seriously damaged and the ecosystem is altered by unregulated human activities. The ecosystem has become more fragile due to deforestation, open grazing, overuse of hill slope mining and riverbed material extraction, unscientific agricultural practices, non-engineered rural roads, and impacts from development projects. These result in landslides, erosion, watershed degradation, loss of wildlife habitat, drying of water sources, loss of fish spawning grounds, aggradation and degradation of riverbed, and desertification of land in Terai due to loss of fertile soil. Hence, the conservation of Chure should be a priority to save it's ecosystem and the fertile lands of Terai. The government has recognized this challenge and prepared the Chure Conservation Master Plan and declared the hills a conservation area.

---

[102] Government of Nepal, Ministry of Home Affairs. 2016. *Disaster Management in Nepal: Status, Achievements, Challenges and Ways Forward. National Position Paper for the Global Platform on Disaster Risk Reduction, 22-26 May 2017, Cancun, Mexico.* Kathmandu.
[103] Government of Nepal, Ministry of Home Affairs. *Nepal Disaster Report 2017: The Road to Sendai.* (Unpublished).
[104] Practical Action. 2017. *Developing National Disaster Risk Reduction Policy and Strategic Action Plan in Nepal 2016–2030: Lessons Learned from Implementation of National Strategy for Disaster Risk Management (NSDRM) 2009.* Kathmandu.

X. RECOMMENDATIONS

The study noted that the many causes of environmental degradation, increased climate change risks and disasters impacting the livelihood of the poor and vulnerable, and incurring huge environmental costs every year were common among the different sectors. Accordingly, the recommendations discussed in the following subsections are grouped as common measures and sector-specific measures. The broad recommendations were reviewed and incorporated in the ADB's new CPS (2020-2024).

A. Common Recommendations

1. Environmental Governance

a. Update, Prepare, and Harmonize National and Subnational Environment Policies

The environment act was updated in 2019, however the regulation require an update to effectively address the environmental safeguards agenda in the context of the new federal structure and the emerging challenges of climate change and disaster risks. The various policies and strategies that have been drafted and lying with MOFE needs to be reviewed in the context of federalization and adopted. An update in the national and subnational policy and regulations for the environment should integrate the lessons learned, define the compliance monitoring and reporting framework, and advise on an effective mechanism for interagency coordination and collaboration. The policy should give clear provision for enforcement of "polluters pay" principle. Sector environment policies and procedures should be prepared or updated following the national and subnational environment policy and regulations. Some of the urgent policy intervention and enforcement required at subnational levels are (i) policy for sustainable operation of mine on riverbed and hill slopes, (ii) minimum environmental requirement for operation of crusher plant; and (iii) working policy for planning and construction of development infrastructure (such as rural roads) with minimal environmental cost.

b. Environmental Mainstreaming in National and Subnational Policies and Programs

Strategic environmental assessments (SEAs) of national and subnational plans, policies, and programs were not mandatory in the past. However, the new environment protection act 2019 has made it necessary prior to implementing government policy and program. SEA is important to be carried out for informed decision-making for safeguarding environment. In the context of current government policy to focus on implementing larger infrastructure developments in energy, transportation, and urban services, the use of the SEA tool has become more pertinent than ever. Priority should be given to conduct SEA of the policy, master plans and strategy of the hydropower, irrigation, transport, urban development, and natural resource management sectors.

c. Strengthen Regional Cooperation for Managing Transboundary Impacts

Environmental impact and climate change risks are transboundary in nature. Hence, a well concerted cooperation is needed among the regional and neighboring countries in addressing the transboundary issues of common interest, such as maintaining migration routes of aquatic biodiversity and corridor of movement of terrestrial wildlife, controlling poaching, managing air and water pollution, and cooperation in integrated water resources management. In this context, and in the context of the formation of provincial and local governments, Nepal should initiate the formulation of legal provisions, management cooperation, and joint monitoring and information sharing within provinces and with the neighboring countries to protect important ecosystem and biodiversity.

2. Institutional Strengthening and Capacity Development

Effective implementation of policies and regulations and environmental governance can be achieved only when government institutions possess sufficient staffing, clear terms of reference, improved capacity, annual plan and program, and adequate financial resources devolved from the national government to the provincial and local levels. Strict enforcement of legal provisions has been a key barrier to effective environmental governance.

The environment protection council and the climate change council are important national safeguards supervisory and policy coordination bodies, which requires reactivation. Under the federal governance system, development responsibilities are decentralized to provincial and local bodies, whereas national planning and policymaking and implementation of major infrastructure projects lie with the central government. Hence, institutional strengthening and capacity building of the Ministry of Forest and Environment (MOFE) and its departments is needed in formulating effective environmental and climate change policy and strategies harmonized with the federal governance system. Strengthening of the safeguard sections of major infrastructure agencies, particularly the energy, urban, transportation, and irrigation sectors is necessary. The newly formed government agencies at the provincial and local levels do not have sufficient structural provision within their organization for addressing environmental safeguards. If a section exists, they are without sufficient human resource and capacity. Hence, institutional strengthening and capacity building support to the safeguard sections of provincial and local municipal bodies is a foremost requirement.

B. Sector Recommendations

1. Sustainable Natural Resources and Land Use Management

a. Combating Watershed Degradation

Large-scale environmental degradation in the hills has occurred due to rampant deforestation, open grazing, watershed encroachment, unchecked hill cutting and deforestation by non-engineered rural road construction, and uncontrolled mining of hill slopes and riverbeds. These have had direct impacts such as watershed degradation, loss of forests and biodiversity, drying of water sources, and landslides in the hills. Flash floods and sediment load have aggraded the rivers in Terai causing devastating floods, bank cutting, desertification of agricultural land, and loss of productivity. The situation is further aggravated by the impact of climate change. The process of degradation has endangered the investments in agriculture and infrastructure development. Support is needed in the implementation of Chure conservation master plan, which aims to control land degradation, protect biodiversity, support livelihood of the communities living in the conversation area, and significantly control the desertification process of fertile agricultural land in Terai. Strict regulation and monitoring by the government, promotion of participatory monitoring, environmentally safe and controlled mining, and introduction of resource pricing and permits for extraction of riverbed aggregates by the local bodies is recommended. Heavy machinery (back-hoe) for constructing non-engineered rural roads on the fragile hills should be restricted. Compensatory plantation should be made mandatory to the infrastructure projects instead of getting away by depositing the required amount in the account of district forest office. Quarries should be closed after completion of work with required protection. Prepare watershed management plans at national level and rollout with decentralized plan for provincial and local governments. Promote the successful example of community management of forests.

b. Sustainable Use of Natural Resources

The government's conservation program needs to be commensurate with the sustainable use of natural resources, including traditional uses by the indigenous communities. Scientific management of forest is required, promoting REDD+ activities and supporting payment for ecosystem services. Use of natural resources and medicinal and aromatic plants needs to be regulated with strict monitoring against undue exploitation. Priority should be given to protecting pollinators, forages, and other forest trees, by promoting agroforestry.[105] Unchecked and over mining of riverbed aggregates should be strictly regularized with community support and government enforcement.

---

[105] Government of Nepal, Ministry of Agriculture Development. 2006. *Agrobiodiversity Policy*. Kathmandu.

c. Biodiversity Conservation

Construction of large-scale projects that cause loss of forest area, human encroachment, and destruction of water bodies threatens Nepal's extremely rich natural resources. Air and water pollution, loss of forests, and the damming of rivers have serious impacts on terrestrial and aquatic biodiversity, with many species becoming critically endangered. Protection of aquatic biodiversity should be prioritized with proper legislation, protection of habitat through strategic planning of dam locations, and proper mitigation measures to protect wildlife movement and fish spawning grounds. Destructive fishing practices should be strictly prohibited through community participation. Infrastructure projects passing through wildlife corridors should introduce wildlife crossings and help affected communities with insurance facility and livelihood support programs associated with nature conservation, such as ecotourism and home-stay programs. Together with ecotourism, market-based instruments can play a significant role in biodiversity conservation, which include taxes, user fees, trust funds, and payment for ecosystem services.

d. Integrated Water Resources Management

Nepal is rich in water resources; however, the resource is underutilized in terms of water supply, irrigation, and energy generation. Some areas within a river basin are water sufficient, but many areas are water deficient. Available water within a basin is also not utilized in a planned and integrated manner due to lack of information, knowledge, and capacity for integrated planning. The federal system of three layers of government has made the situation more complicated on equitable sharing and integrated management of the natural resources. The draft IWRM policy, act, and regulation, of which preparation is led by the Water and Energy Commission (WEC), should be updated in the context of federalism and natural resource sharing between provinces and local bodies. A strategic environmental assessment of the policy should be conducted. An efficient governance could achieve improved water security by aiming for an updated national water policy, efficient institutional arrangement at all three tiers of government, equitable sharing of water, and capacity to operationalize IWRM needs.

e. River Conservation

Most of the urban rivers of Nepal have become highly polluted, particularly from direct discharge of household wastewater and solid waste. They require cleaning up with revival of riverine ecosystem, and augmentation of dry season flow. ADB is supporting the government in improving the environment of the Bagmati and other rivers in capital city through large-scale investments in wastewater infrastructure, including interceptor sewers, wastewater treatment plants, river corridor beautification, and water flow augmentation in Bagmati during the dry season. Similar interventions are required for other polluted rivers in other urban centers. Few industries are polluting water bodies by directly discharging untreated effluent into the rivers (Bagmati, Narayani, and East Rapti rivers). Such illegal practices must be restricted with strict monitoring and enforcement. The government's capacity for meaningful monitoring could be enhanced through community participation. Dedicated river basin organizations should be established to ensure basin-wide water use management with environment protection.

2. Sustainable Infrastructure Development

a. Common Issues in Sustainable Infrastructure Development

There are safeguard issues that are crosscutting and common across infrastructure development projects. The common issues and recommendations are outlined below.

- Update old standards, policies, acts, and regulations to promote environment friendly, climate- proof, and disaster-resilient infrastructure.
- Non-compliance in projects are generally found to be due to ignorance of the contractor on their safeguard responsibilities or negligence as a result of unclear scope and payment for their services for complying with the environment management plan. Hence, the EMP requirements should always be a part of the tender document, with activities and cost listed in the BOQ.
- Make contractual requirement for contractors to submit site-specific environment management plan for employer's approval before mobilizing in the field.
- A general practice by the government is to include few generic sentences on safeguard requirements in the

contract agreements, which does not give much room for the employer to enforce contractors to comply with safeguard requirements; thus, contractors easily get away with non-compliance. Hence, the contract agreement document should include detailed and clear safeguard clauses including reward and punish mechanism.

- Arrange sufficient input of environment expert in projects, depending on the environmental significance and size and type of projects.
- Development projects have universally suffered due to delay in getting clearance for cutting trees to work in a forest area. Hence, a one-window mechanism to assess, issue clearance of, and monitor tree cutting and compensatory plantation could be an efficient mechanism to expedite the issue.
- Make tree plantation by development projects not only a compensatory measure but an additional activity to improve green cover.
- Establish "forest bank" by major infrastructure development agencies for readily compensating forest area and trees cleared by development projects.

b. Sustainable Transportation

A sustainable transportation system minimizes the use of land and the generation of GHG emissions, waste, and noise by following "avoid–shift–improve" principle. "Avoid" guides for shortening travel; "shift" guides for changing to more energy efficient modes (such as promoting cycle, footpath, walkways, and efficient and time saving routes); and "improve" means using technologies that are less polluting and more energy efficient. The recommendations for sustainable transport are:

- Update the Nepal Road Standard (2014) and related acts and regulations by making mandatory to consider the non-motorized transport infrastructure such as pedestrian zones and footpaths, zebra crossing, walkways (sky walk), dedicated cycle tracks, and cycle parking spots.
- Standardize climate and disaster resilient design of transport infrastructure and ensure its mainstreaming in strategic and rural road standards for design and implementation.
- Introduce mandatory requirement to install noise barriers at important and sensitive places, sufficient and appropriate delineators, sign boards, road safety

sign, road direction boards, traffic signs, roadside tree plantation, and mandatory compensatory plantation in the right of way; and enforce them through act and regulation.

- Allocate a separate environment cost in new road construction and annual road maintenance budget for establishing nursery, undertaking plantation and their guarding.
- Encourage road safety through institutional mechanisms, such as independent road safety agency (a road safety strategy is in draft stage awaiting government's approval).
- Prioritize "road maintenance" in all type of roads.
- Promote modes of transport with low energy emission, such as the use of manual or electric vehicles, railways, and inland waterways.
- Support in formulating policies and establishing or operationalizing safeguard section in the federal, provincial, and local government institutions in major infrastructure development sectors and support in their capacity development.
- Support planning and implementation of sustainable urban transportation plan including improvements in public transportation system.
- Conduct strategic environmental assessment (SEA) of transport sector policies and plans.

c. Sustainable Urban Development

Sustainable urban development helps in improving urban mobility and access to public health, while reducing air and water pollution. The recommendations for promoting sustainable urban development are:

- Support updating of existing policy and harmonize the urban policy and legal provisions among federal, provincial, and local governments.
- Approve and implement national pollution control strategy and action plan, and plan for minimizing carbon emission (draft prepared awaiting government's approval).
- Support upcoming towns and urban centers in preparing sustainable and climate resilient urban development master plans to avoid unplanned growth devoid of basic urban amenities.
- Establish and strengthen safeguard sections in federal, provincial, and local government institutions with

sufficient staff and resources, and full authority and accountability to enforce policies and regulations.

- Promote use of clean energy with lower carbon emissions in urban areas.
- Mainstream climate change and disaster risks in various aspects of urban development including preparing plan for settlements (compact and energy efficient) and infrastructures (transport, energy, water supply and sanitation, and waste management).
- Promote urban open areas, urban greenery, "room to play," and sponge cities for risk reduction.
- Reduce greenhouse gas and air pollution by translocating polluting industries including brick kilns, shifting to clean energy (electric or solar) vehicles, and managing solid waste.
- Support urban areas in establishing climate friendly solid waste management and wastewater treatment.
- Promote public awareness in environment friendly practices, such as minimizing the use of plastic bags and waste generation, recycling waste, and avoiding open discharge of wastewater in the rivers.
- Establish a system of conducting SEA of key plans, strategies, and programs on sustainable urban development.
- Prepare knowledge products from past experience and replicate good lessons learned from country and regional experience.

d. Clean Energy Development

Nepal has aimed to generate 3,000 MW in 3 years; 5,000 MW in 5 years; and 15,000 MW of electricity in the next 10 years. The major risk lies in serious environmental degradation in a rush to develop infrastructures. Recommendations for clean energy development are:

- Strengthen safeguard sections in the ministry, department, and Nepal Electricity Authority at federal level. Support institution and capacity building of federal, provincial, and local governments in environment friendly and climate resilient development, particularly in reinforcing systematic compliance, monitoring, and enforcement system.
- Study the impact of ad hoc placing of dams on rivers—which block fish passage and cause almost no downstream release for environment flow—to sustain aquatic biodiversity in new and existing hydropower and irrigation projects.

- Review the action plan suggested by ADB's Nepal Energy Sector Assessment, Strategy and Roadmap 2017, and implement environmental safeguards recommendations rather than attempting to make safeguard provisions flexible.
- Encourage renewable and alternative low-carbon energy sources, such as hydro, solar, and wind energy. Promote off-grid, community-based micro- hydro and solar power systems.
- Conduct strategic environmental assessment (SEA) of energy sector plans and policies.
- Prepare transmission line master plan with SEA and use existing transmission line corridors with multiple stringing as a common right of way instead of constructing multiple parallel lines through the forests.
- Promote regional coordination (such as in protecting migratory routes of fishes and other aquatic biodiversity along interconnected river basins) with neighboring countries to manage transboundary impacts.
- Promote public awareness on environment friendly practices such as minimizing the use of energy and switching to renewable energy.
- Prepare knowledge products from past experience and replicate good lessons learned from country and regional experience.

3. Strengthening Environmental Governance and Management Capacity

Environmental governance has become the most pertinent challenge in the context of three levels of governments established under federalization. The federal government ministries and departments may have some level of institutional arrangement and capacity for safeguards, but the same institutions at the provincial and local levels are extremely weak. The recommendations proposed are:

a. Policy and Institutional Framework

(i) Policy Formulation and Update
- Update or formulate policies, acts, regulations, and strategies to address gaps in the existing system and make them relevant under the newly formed federal structure of governance.
- Support provincial and local bodies in formulating local policies that are environment friendly and resilient to the risks of climate change, and in promoting forest

and biodiversity conservation. The legal provisions should make public monitoring and enforcement mandatory. Such arrangement should be legally binding by integrating it with environment protection act and regulation (new environment protection act 2019 has made SEA mandatory for all government policy and programs published in gazette).

- Adopt stringent policy to enforce action on haphazard and environment damaging construction practices, such as non-engineered and machine-led road constructions in the hills, ad hoc placing of dams across rivers causing barrier to fish migration, aligning infrastructure through the forests along wildlife movement corridors, and overexploitation of rivers to extract construction material.
- Review and update sector infrastructure design standards to make them climate resilient and environment friendly, particularly for transportation, urban, energy, and water resources sectors.
- Adopt and implement REDD+ strategy, Nepal biodiversity strategy and action plan, forestry sector policy, Chure master plan, emission reduction program, national pollution control strategy and action plan, and low carbon economic development strategy.
- Establish regional cooperation and understanding with neighboring countries on transboundary environmental management issues.

(ii) Institutional Strengthening

- Establish fully resourced and functional safeguard institutions with full staffing and budget within all three levels of government. Support them to build capacity in environmental governance, monitoring, and enforcement.
- Establish a system of stronger and closer stakeholder engagement and inter-government coordination, especially for complex projects with challenging safeguard issues.
- Build negotiation capacity of communities in marketing natural resource conservation and carbon sequestration for economic benefits through payment for ecosystem services.
- Prepare national, environmental, and natural resource database and operationalize national environmental management information system for informed decision-making.

b. Compliance and Enforcement

- Strengthen environment protection regulation for pollution and compliance monitoring with punitive actions on defaulters ("polluter pay" principle). Identify agencies responsible for monitoring and enforcement at national, provincial, and local levels, and prepare working directives to guide the process of monitoring, recording, and reporting. Adopt participatory monitoring systems.
- Keep EMP compliance requirements in contractor's bill of quantities and detailed provision in the contract agreement document. Prepare standard BOQ items and contract agreement clauses to facilitate enforcement by executing and implementing agencies.
- Continue and build upon the successful results of nature conservation management such as the highly successful participatory community forest management, participatory buffer zone management, leasehold forestry, eco-guardians, and buffer zone management committees.
- Build on the conservation efforts for highly vulnerable ecological zones, such as Chure Hills.
- Maintain biological passes and inclusion of wildlife viaducts in wildlife corridors. Install vigilance through CC camera for speed restriction and identification of vehicles involved in wildlife hit and run cases.
- Prepare plan and implement compensatory plantation program from the beginning of project implementation. Grow saplings in nursery for a few years to make them mature before transplanting.
- Major infrastructure development agencies may buy land around the forest area, plant trees, and keep as "land and tree bank" to use in future as replacement during compensatory measure.
- Pilot the use of "fish screening framework" prepared by ADB and follow up to link with the government's environment protection regulation.[106]

4. Responding to Climate Change Imperative

Climate related natural hazards such as floods, landslides, droughts, and extreme weather events are increasing in

106 D.B. Singh and D.B. Swar. 2018. *Impact of Dam on Fish in the Rivers of Nepal.* Manila: Asian Development Bank.

severity and frequency, causing loss of lives and property. The communities face climate costs due to their fragile geophysical structures, unplanned and unsafe settlements, environmental degradation, and low adaptive capacity. The federal government ministries and departments may have some level of institutional arrangement and capacity, but the same institutions at the provincial and local levels are extremely weak. The recommendations on responding to climate change risks are:

- Support strengthening of climate change risk assessment capacity at national, provincial, and local levels. Establish fully resourced and functional climate change units with staffing and budget at all three levels of government across sectors.
- Update policies, acts, regulations, and strategies on climate change to make them relevant under the newly formed federal governance. Provincial and local bodies require support in formulating local policies that are climate and disaster resilient and environment friendly.
- Strengthen public sector capacity in mainstreaming climate change risks in the project cycle to climate proof infrastructures. Embed climate change risks at all stages of project processing through risk screening and assessment of climate change impact, vulnerability, and adaptation.
- Upscale indigenous knowledge of vulnerable communities on adaptation to the risks of climate change.[107]
- The present hydrometeorological stations are not sufficient and technically capable to measure the spatial and temporal variation in temperature, rainfall, and other elements of atmosphere. Hence, invest on adding stations and improve technical quality of data collection by using advanced technology, and support capacity building.
- Improve climatic data collection and analysis, and knowledge dissemination to farmers, researchers, and decision-makers.
- Invest on applied research on economic footprint of climate change on national economy, and prepare plan for climate-resilient agriculture under the umbrella of the government's agriculture development strategy.
- Use multimodal transport system, such as rural roads, ropeway, suspension bridge, and trail bridge for access readiness to combat the impacts of climate-change-induced disasters.
- Collaborate with agencies researching on GLOF (ICIMOD), identify the most vulnerable river basins to GLOF, and prepare measures to minimize risks and protect infrastructure. Prepare safety plan along with early warning system and evacuation plan.
- Promote activities that capitalize on ecosystem-inherent resilience to natural risks to protect and enhance livelihoods.
- Focus on restoration of damaged ecosystems to build resilience against disaster risks.
- Support the Department of Hydrology and Meteorology in preparing database on climate indicators.
- Update and make climate change policy, NAPA, and LAPA applicable in the context of a federal governance system. Implement recommendations of NAPA and LAPA.
- Initiate regional consultation, cooperation, agreements, and strategic partnership, and complement them with legal provisions, such as memorandum of understanding.
- Promote watershed conservation, and forest and natural resource management to maximize carbon sequestration, and bring them to the international market for payment for ecosystem services (PES).
- Discourage use of fossil fuel and encourage use of clean renewable energy through market-based incentives.
- Promote access to financial instruments, such as climate investment fund, global environment facility, green climate fund, and ADB's climate change fund, for climate change adaptation and resilience building as planned under NAPA and LAPA.
- Prepare knowledge products from past experience and replicate good lessons learned from country and regional experience.

---

[107] Government of Nepal, Ministry of Science, Technology, and Environment. 2015. *Indigenous and Local Knowledge and Practices for Climate Resilience in Nepal: Mainstreaming Climate Change Risk Management in Development.* Kathmandu.

C. Recommendations Considered by the New Country Partnership Strategy for Nepal 2020-2024

ADB's Environmental Operational Directions 2013–2020 calls for promoting transitions to green growth under the three pillars of building sustainable infrastructure, investing in natural capital, and improving environmental governance by mainstreaming climate change risks in all stages of planning and development. This was also validated by the cause-and-effect and mitigation analysis conducted by this study. ADB Strategy 2030 focuses on poverty alleviation, tackling climate change, building climate and disaster resilience, and enhancing environmental sustainability. Following ADB's strategy and operational directives and complementing the government's periodic plan, ADB continues to support Nepal in the areas of environmental protection, adaptation and resilience to climate change, and disaster risks management. ADB aims to support Nepal in the following broad areas through the new CPS.

1. Improved Environmental Governance

ADB during the current CPS period supported the government in establishing environmental safeguard unit in Project Management Directorate of Nepal Electricity Authority; Project Implementation Directorate of the Kathmandu Upatyaka Khanipani Limited; and Department of Water Resources and Irrigation; and in formulating sector guidelines on environment. ADB also supported in drafting national pollution control strategy and action plan, and capacity building of government agencies in mainstreaming climate change risks in their operation. The guidelines and strategy require updating to harmonize with the new federal governance system. The newly formed local governments are unprepared in terms of institutional set-up, resources and staffing, and effective policy to combat climate change, disaster, and environmental challenges. Recommendations considered by the new CPS are:

- Support the activation of existing safeguard units/sections and establish new safeguard sections in key infrastructure ministry/department of federal, provincial, and local governance.
- Support in enforcement of the new environment act (2019) taking into account the federal government

system and the emerging issues such as climate change and transboundary impacts.
- Support strengthening of country safeguard system through updating national and sector environmental policies and regulations integrating environmental and climate change factors.
- Explore the potential use of the integrated flood-risk management—a part of nature- based solution—in weather-related disasters.
- Densification and land use planning are critically important for sustainable urban development. Hence, support capacity building of local and provincial governments and promote use of various planning tools to prepare and implement integrated urban development.
- Extend ADB support to provincial and local governments in policy formulation, guidelines preparation, institutional strengthening, and capacity building.
- Support in adoption of the national pollution control strategy and action plan prepared under ADB support.
- Formulate new strategy for solid waste management involving resource recovery and waste reduction, participatory methods in land management, and penalties for open dumping or burning of waste.
- Prepare procedural guidelines and occupational health and safety manual for implementing development works in order to minimize pollution, ensure safety, and reduce hardships to people.
- Support the preparation of strategic environmental assessment (SEA) and conduct SEA of important sector plan, policy, and program, as also envisaged by new environment protection act 2019.

Climate Change Adaptation and Resilience

ADB has supported Nepal in addressing the impacts of climate change through a strategic program for climate resilience in coordination with Climate Investment Fund. Technical assistance in climate-resilient planning and project implementation was provided for 12 government agencies to mainstream climate change risks in their operation. ADB is also supporting the communities affected by the seriously water-stressed basins by augmenting water source through watershed conservation and providing water access to the communities under Building Climate

Resilience of Watersheds in Mountain Eco-Regions. Recommendations considered by the new CPS are:

- Support in institutional strengthening and capacity development of all three levels of governments in climate-resilient planning, design and implementation. Also orient them on innovative climate change financing and risk-sharing approaches.
- Ensure climate proofing is embedded in the project cycle beginning with risk screening and, if required, conduct a detailed climate impact, vulnerability, and adaptation assessment.
- Scale-up the use of alternative and renewable energy and reduce fossil fuel dependency.
- Support Nepal in targeting investments in resilience building of poor communities, women, and vulnerable groups.
- Promote expansion and use of clean energy and sustainable infrastructure development to minimize GHG emission.
- Support watershed and forest conservation for increased carbon sequestration, and link with REDD+ to strengthen the capacity of government and community in negotiation for payment for ecosystem services in the international market.
- Seek partnership with development partners and climate change support funds to leverage investments in climate change adaptation and resilience building.
- Develop knowledge products on climate change adaptation and resilience for wider dissemination.

3. Sustainable Infrastructure Developent

ADB has supported Nepal in building strategic and rural roads, transmission lines and renewable energies, urban development, and agriculture and irrigation. The ADB-supported infrastructures generally included environment friendly and climate-resilient design, compensatory plantation, and biodiversity protection. The use of electric vehicles was piloted (under the South Asia Tourism Infrastructure Development Project) and footpaths were constructed (under the Kathmandu Sustainable Urban Transport Project). Following are the recommendations considered by the new CPS.

- Support updating or preparation of road, energy, urban, and irrigation standards, policies, and master plans at all

three levels of government for a planned and integrated infrastructure development.
- Promote low-carbon and climate-resilient development such as non-motorized and carbon-neutral transportation (cycles, walkways, skyways, electric vehicles, ropeways, railways, and waterways).
- Practice saving trees (to the extent possible), adopt mandatory compensatory plantation by the project, and dampen noise in sensitive locations, such as settlements, schools, hospitals, and religious/heritage sites such as beside the Lumbini World Heritage Site where the SASEC Road Improvement Project is implemented.
- Promote green and smart roads not only for enhanced connectivity, but also for water management and flood protection.
- Encourage participatory solid waste and wastewater management for rapidly growing urban centers through Regional Urban Development Project.
- Integrate open space and greening into urban infrastructure design from the beginning to provide more public open space (which has resilience benefits for emergencies), mitigate urban heat island effect, reduce air pollution, and enhance quality of life and develop sponge cities to tackle flood.
- Conduct SEA of sector development plan and policies, including hydropower policy 2011 (irrigation master plan being prepared under ADB support), the 20-year Agriculture Development Strategy 2015, and the proposed strategic road master plan.
- Adopt the "avoid-shift-improve" principle of sustainable transport development.
- Control non-engineered, machine-based rural road constructions, and support road maintenance in addition to new road construction (Rural Connectivity Improvement Project). Regulate movement of heavy vehicle and tractors on rural earthen roads during monsoon.
- Promote strategic partnership with regional organizations, such as Global Environment Facility, UN agencies, and knowledge-based agencies (WWF and International Union for Conservation of Nature) in sustainable infrastructure development.
- Support capacity building and institutional strengthening of federal, provincial, and local governments in environment friendly and climate-resilient planning and implementation.

- Develop knowledge products on sustainable infrastructure development for wider dissemination.

4. Investing in Natural Capital

In the last CPS period, ADB supported Nepal in reviving polluted urban water bodies (i.e., Bagmati River in Kathmandu) through water augmentation, natural treatment, riverbank beautification, solid waste management, watershed conservation, and awareness generation. The integrated water resources management (IWRM) policy and act is under preparation (ADB Water Resources Project Preparatory Facility). Establishing a river basin organization will be supported for river basin-wide integrated water management through Bagmati River Basin Improvement Project (BRBIP) and BRBIP-Additional Financing. The SASEC Road Connectivity Project supported in building elephant underpass and mobilizing communities in eco-tourism activities. SASEC Road Improvement Project and SASEC Highway Improvement Project is planning to construct wildlife crossings in the buffer zone of Chitwan National Park and Parsa Wildlife National Park. Recommendations considered by the new CPS are:

- Apply the lessons learned in natural resources conservation from BRBIP and SASEC Road Connectivity Project in new projects (SASEC Road Improvement Project, SASEC Highway Improvement Project, and BRBIP second phase).
- Continue to mainstream environmental sustainability and disaster resilience in the design of infrastructure projects.
- Urgently adopt the IWRM policy, act, and regulations supported by Water Resources Project Preparatory Facility, which is harmonized with natural resource sharing mechanism under the federal system.
- The BRBIP and BRBIP-Additional Financing shall continue to support the establishment of a river basin organization for Bagmati River.
- Use nature-based solutions that can provide sustainable and cost-effective options with multiple benefits from restoring ecosystems to promote sustainable urbanization, improving risk management, and addressing climate change.

- Promote beneficiary stakeholder participation in the management of natural resources at all levels.
- Rehabilitate watersheds with participatory involvement of local communities (strengthen community forest user group, water user association of farmers).
- Support Nepal in addressing the serious environmental degradation and disaster risks posed by overexploitation of the natural resources of Chure Hills under the Chure Conservation Master Plan. Conduct SEA of the master plan.
- Promote compensatory tree plantation and greening of roads by making it mandatory in Nepal Road Standard and legal provisions of other sectors. Prepare tree cutting and compensatory plantation manual.
- Promote wildlife protection and support ecosystem-based initiatives (i.e., animal pass, ecotourism, and home stay to reduce human-wildlife conflicts.
- Adopt strategic planning of dam locations and proper mitigation measures to protect fish migratory routes and spawning grounds. Pilot the use of "fish screening framework." [108]
- Support all three levels of government in adoption of pollution control and enforcement of policies.
- Provide technical support in conducting research studies on environment protection, climate resilience, natural resources and biodiversity management.
- Promote regional cooperation to enhance the effectiveness of transboundary environmental initiatives and biodiversity conservation.
- Develop knowledge products on natural capital investment.

5. Disaster Risk Management

ADB has supported the government in preparing digitized water induced hazard maps of 25 major river basins, participatory approaches in disaster prevention, preparedness, and rehabilitation, and a mechanism for effective cooperation and coordination among stakeholders. ADB is also supporting in earthquake-resistant and safer schools, community buildings, and improving access to facilitate post-disaster relief supply through earthquake emergency assistance project. Recommendations considered by the new CPS are:

---

[108] See footnote 106.

- Formulate measures and instruments that can reduce disaster risk in an efficient and sustainable manner. These should draw upon "hard" structural measures (physical interventions), "soft" structural measures (such as room for the river), non-structural measures (such as flood forecast and early warnings), and policy instruments (such as land use planning and insurance).
- Prioritize community involvement in planning and implementing a community-based risk management plan at the local level. ADB will consider reducing community vulnerability through flood protection, flood forecasting and early warning systems, and post-disaster shelters in vulnerable areas (particularly in flood vulnerable areas of Terai) through Tanahu Hydropower Project, Priority River Basin Flood Risk Management Project, and Dudhkoshi Hydropower Project in addition to others.
- Investment support for construction of safer schools with "build back better" principle will be continued (Disaster Resilience of Schools Project).
- Support in ensuring improved access to remote areas in the event of disaster and timely relief supply and evacuation through improved connectivity (Earthquake Emergency Assistance Project; Rural Connectivity Improvement Project).

- Prepare river basin profile and flood maps for categorizing critical flood risk areas to support in planning flood protection measures and safer land use.
- Adopt nature-based solutions and encourage the concepts of wetland promotion, "room for the river," sponge cities for risk reduction, cost savings, and investment optimization (Priority River Basin Flood Risk Management Project).
- Manage flood risks and support in informed decision-making on investment.
- Support a comprehensive approach to disaster risk financing and post-disaster budget and execution capabilities.

6. Knowledge Management
- Strengthen knowledge and institutional capabilities of all three tiers of government through training in environmental protection, climate change adaptation, and disaster risk management.
- Prepare knowledge products from past experience and replicate good lessons learned from country and regional experience. Share knowledge within and outside ADB.

www.ingramcontent.com/pod-product-compliance
Lightning Source LLC
Chambersburg PA
CBHW061224270326
41927CB00025B/3491